The Study of Religions

OTHER BOOKS BY JEAN HOLM

Teaching Religion in School
New Movements in Religious Education (Contributor)

The Study of Religions

Jean Holm

A CROSSROAD BOOK
The Seabury Press
New York

1977
The Seabury Press
815 Second Avenue
New York, N.Y. 10017

Printed in the United States of America

Library of Congress Cataloging in Publication Data

Holm, Jean, 1922-   The study of religions.
"A Crossroad book."
Includes index.
1. Religions—Study and teaching.   I. Title.
BL41.H625   1977   200'.7   76-15426   ISBN 0-8164-1227-8

CONTENTS

General editors of this book
and others in
the *Issues in Religious Studies* series:
Peter Baelz and Jean Holm

Part 1

QUESTIONS OF SCOPE

1

APPROACHING THE STUDY

In the early days of the Christian Church many people in the Roman Empire believed that Christians practised cannibalism when they gathered together week by week for their secret meetings. After all, didn't their rites include eating flesh and drinking blood?

In the Middle Ages many Christians believed that Jews sacrificed a Christian child at Passover time and used its blood in the making of unleavened bread.

These are two rather crude examples of the misunderstanding of other men's religions which has been widespread throughout most of human history. Religious activity of one kind or another would appear to be as old as mankind but there has been remarkably little attempt to find out about other men's beliefs and practices, and it was not until the nineteenth century that any systematic study of religions was undertaken.

Popular interest in learning about other religions is an even more recent development. There are many reasons for this. More people can now visit countries where other religions are practised. Television programmes show us the customs, the worship and the festivals of other peoples. Adherents of other faiths have come to live among us. Many, especially the young, have been attracted by the meditation techniques of Eastern religions. But the most significant reason is probably the growth of Religious Studies in schools, colleges and universities.

Traditionally, in the West, names such as Theology and Religious Instruction have been used for courses consisting of the study of the Christian faith—and no one thought it neces-sary to describe the courses as Christian Theology or Instruction in the Christian Religion. Where other religions were included at all they were regarded as extra to the main syllabus. Some university faculties of theology have had optional papers in one or more of the major religions, and a number of schools have

1

had courses in the Comparative Study of Religions as part of sixth-form religious education.

The name Religious Studies indicates a different approach from that of Theology. The emphasis is put on the study of religion as a human phenomenon, and the student may be an adherent of any faith or of none. The concept of religion, however, is an abstraction; we can't look around us and see 'religion', for religion is found only in the form of particular religions, so religious studies involves us in a study of religions. If we study just one of them we may well get an unbalanced picture of what religion is. For instance, many Christians think that religion necessarily involves a belief in a supreme Being, a form of congregational worship and a set of credal statements. Theravāda Buddhism is one religion which does not conform to this pattern.[1] As we shall see, there are wide variations among religions, and it is important to recognize both the differences and the similarities.

HOW DO WE START?

The study of religions is not to be undertaken lightly. It is a tremendously demanding exercise. Few of us have anything like a thorough knowledge of our own religious tradition. How then is it possible to gain an adequate understanding of other people's traditions? Alexander Pope's warning about the dangers of 'a little learning' certainly applies to the study of religions, for a superficial knowledge can be completely misleading. So what do we do? Do we concentrate on only one other religion besides our own?

In the academic study of religions there have been two main schools of thought. One has argued that the study of one religion is a lifetime's work for a professional researcher. He must learn the language (or languages) of that religion

---

[1] It is non-theistic, i.e. it is not concerned with the question of the existence of God or gods. The Buddha said that gods have nothing to do with man's salvation and man should therefore not waste time thinking about them. Thus there is no worship in the sense in which we understand it, and the meditation which in Theravāda Buddhism takes the place of worship is a private and individual matter. There are beliefs, like those expressed in the Four Supreme Truths, but they are an analysis of man's condition, not theological statements.

thoroughly, he must soak himself in its culture, he must spend some time living in the country (or countries) where it is practised, he must acquire a detailed knowledge of its scriptures and traditions, and he must become familiar with all aspects of its belief and practice, both in the present and throughout its history.

The other school of thought maintains that the undeniable advantages of specializing in one religious tradition are outweighed by the advantages to be gained from a comparative approach. This usually involves the study of particular aspects of belief and practice in a number of religions, aspects such as mythology, or initiation rites, or concepts of time, or beliefs about life after death. Among those who have worked in this way is Mircea Eliade, the Romanian-born History of Religions professor at the University of Chicago. His books have titles like *The Sacred and the Profane*; *Myths, Dreams and Mysteries*; *Images and Symbols*, and *Birth and Rebirth*. This second school of thought claims that only a cross-cultural study can really lead to an understanding of what religion is.

Although this debate belongs in the higher reaches of academic scholarship it serves as a useful reminder of the vastness of the field we are entering, and of the care with which any study must be tackled if it is to be of value.

People will have different reasons for learning about religions. Some will want to find out more about a particular religion because they have visited a country where it is practised or because they have got to know members of that faith. Some will have the pattern of their study prescribed by the examination syllabus they are following, with a paper devoted to a major living religion or perhaps a paper demanding a cross-cultural study in two or more religions of topics like worship, or man and his destiny, or sacred writings. Those whose main interest is in exploring the nature of religion will want to undertake the study of more than one religion. But which?

Many of the books we have easy access to purport to be about 'world religions' or 'the living religions of mankind'. They are likely to include Hinduism, Buddhism, Judaism and Islam, and perhaps Shinto and Confucianism. If we stop to think about this selection we become aware of some interesting facts. In the first place these religions originated in, and are still mainly found in, the Middle East, the Indian continent and Asia. Vast areas of the world, e.g. Oceania, South America and most of Africa, are excluded.

Secondly, even in the Middle East, the Indian continent and Asia there are many more religions than the six listed. Jainism, which developed out of Hinduism at about the same time as Buddhism (sixth century B.C.), occasionally gets a passing mention, but Sikhism, which was shaped by both Hindu and Muslim beliefs in the sixteenth century A.D., is often completely ignored; and although Taoism has been much more influential than Confucianism in the lives of ordinary people in China—and has in many ways a greater claim to be called a religion—it has no guarantee of a place among what have been called 'world religions'.

Thirdly, the impression is created that there is only a small number of religions in the world. It is true that there are not many which number their adherents in hundreds of millions, but is size the only factor that makes a religion worth studying? Once we have included the traditional religions of tribal peoples we find that there are literally thousands of religions. Many of them exist in the countries represented in the conventional selection of world religions as well as in those parts of the world which are normally neglected in the study of religions. There are, for example, numerous tribal religions in the Indian continent. Partly because of our lack of knowledge of them we have tended to lump together, quite unjustifiably, all traditional religions (also called primal or primitive religions; see p. 35). They often have features in common but most of them have their own quite distinctive pattern of beliefs and practices.[2] It would be like saying that Judaism, Christianity and Islam are only one religion because they share a number of beliefs.

Fourthly, the conventional list of religions leaves out Christianity. Does it not count as a world religion? The writers of the kind of book we have been discussing assumed that their readers were Christian and that they therefore needed to learn only about other faiths. However, being an adherent of a religion is quite a different kind of activity from studying it as one religion alongside other religions.

It would be absurd to suggest that we should ignore the conventional list of world religions, but on the other hand we

[2] See John Mbiti, *African Religions and Philosophy*. Heinemann 1969.

4

should not just accept it unthinkingly. We have to ask which would be the best religions for *us* to study.

It makes sense to consider first the religions which are represented in our part of the world. Quite apart from the purposes of our academic study it is interesting to know something about the faith of people whom we are likely to come across in our country or, more widely, in our region. To call this 'interesting', however, is to put it at its lowest. We *ought* to know something about the faith of such people. Religions are not optional hobbies, like stamp collecting or fishing, which people turn to in their spare time. They affect the way a person understands the world and how he lives, and they are closely related to his sense of identity. If we don't know anything about Islam we cannot hope to understand Muslims.

In some countries adherents of other faiths have arrived comparatively recently. In others they have been there for centuries. They may have been there before the arrival of the Christian population. This would be true, for example, of the Indians in the American continent and the Maoris in New Zealand. Where religious communities have been established for a considerable period they are likely to have contributed to the culture of the country as, for example, the Jews have in Europe.

Another reason for studying religions which are represented in our own country or region is that we have access to much more valuable resource material. It is easier to get hold of literature published by adherents of these religions, and we may be able to meet and talk with people, attend their places of worship, visit the shops that cater for their needs, and even take part in their festivals.

If we accept this criterion of nearness, students in Britain will consider first the religions of the main immigrant groups— Hindu, Muslim and Sikh—and the long-established Jewish community, and they will note that there is a small number of Buddhists, mainly of the Theravāda and Zen schools. Students in the U.S.A. will compile a different list. It will certainly include Judaism, because there are more Jews living in America than in all the other countries put together, but it will probably include Chinese and Japanese religions, and it will certainly include the indigenous Indian religious traditions.

In Australasia the pattern will be different again, with the inclusion of the religious traditions of the peoples of the South

5

Pacific and those of the Australian aboriginals. The historical religions, apart from Christianity, are not widely represented in Australia and New Zealand, but these countries belong to the community of nations which stretches right up the West Pacific to Japan, and in this area there are Shinto, several schools of Buddhism, Taoism, the tribal religions of South-East Asia, Islam in Indonesia and Hinduism in Fiji.

Similarly, South Africa belongs to the African community, with its wealth of tribal religions, its nations which are wholly or partly Muslim, and the numerous communities of Hindus and Muslims living in the countries along the east coast of the continent.

We have assumed in the preceding paragraphs that the cultural background of the student (using the term 'student' in its widest sense) is Christian and that he is considering which other religions to study. Where his main interest is in understanding the nature of religion he should of course include Christianity. Not only will the knowledge of it with which he has grown up give him a flying start in interpreting what he discovers as his study deepens, but he can also observe the religion in practice in the society around him.

GETTING THE BALANCE RIGHT

Where one of the main purposes of our study is to understand the nature of religion we have to ask whether the religions represented in our country or region provide a broad enough cross-section. For instance, if the only religions in an area were Christianity, Islam and Judaism the selection would be too narrow. We might well conclude from our studies that all religions included a belief in a personal God, who had created the world and who had certain moral attributes. We might also conclude that all religions believed that God had revealed his will to man, and that this revelation was enshrined in the form of scriptures.

If we want to choose religions which illustrate significant variations we might use the following questions as guidelines:

Does it have an historical founder (as in Buddhism, Christianity, Islam, Sikhism) or is there no known founder (as in Hinduism, Judaism, Shinto, and traditional religions)?

6

Does it have authoritative scriptures (as in the monotheistic religions and Theravāda Buddhism), does it regard its sacred writings as authoritative but not revealed by a personal God (as in Hinduism and most of the Mahāyāna Buddhist schools), does it reject scriptures (as in Zen), or is it a non-literate religion, with a store of oral traditions (as in primal religions)?

Is its belief about God uncompromisingly monotheistic (as in Islam and Judaism), does it believe that God has manifested himself in a human life (as in Christianity and Vaishnavite Hinduism), or that he is manifest in aspects of nature (as in some traditional religions), or is it non-theistic (as in Theravāda Buddhism)?

Does it believe that it has the truth for all men, and therefore encourages conversion (as in Christianity, Islam and Buddhism), does it believe that all religions are paths to the truth (as in Hinduism), or does it assume that one is born into a religion (as in tribal religions and, to a certain extent, Judaism)?

It must not be thought that the beliefs of the religions which have been bracketed together in this way are identical. The Hindu Vaishnavite belief in the incarnation of the God Vishnu, for example, is quite different from the Christian belief in the incarnation of God in the person of Jesus Christ (see page 42). The grouping serves merely to illustrate relatively similar approaches and to give some guidance for the task of choosing areas of study.

2

DEFINING RELIGION

Studying religion sounds like a fairly straightforward activity—until we ask how we are to define religion. Defining means 'drawing a line round', so that we can distinguish what comes within the boundary from what lies outside it.

In the past some people tried to answer the question 'What is religion?' by offering theories about how it originated. Some of these theories were psychological, suggesting that religion was a projection of primitive man's mental state—fear, frustration, guilt, etc.—or that early man ascribed personality to such powerful natural phenomena as the sun, moon, stars and wind, or that the appearance in dreams of members of the tribe who had died led men to believe in the existence of spirits. The most well-known name associated with psychological theories is that of Sigmund Freud (1856–1939).

Other theories of the origin of religion were sociological, suggesting that religious beliefs and practices developed because societies needed sanctions to make their members conform to a way of life which would give stability to the social group and increase its well-being, or that what primitive man worshipped was society itself, represented by the clan or tribe totem. The first great exponent of this kind of theory was the French sociologist, Émile Durkheim (1858–1917).[1]

A large number of psychological and sociological theories were put forward in the last half of the nineteenth century and the first two or three decades of this one, but although many of the men who offered them made important contributions in other ways to our understanding of religion, all theories about its origin have long since been discredited. One reason, among others, is that they could never be more than speculations. Because they dealt with remote prehistoric time—'in the beginning'—it would be impossible to prove, or to disprove,

[1] See further E. E. Evans-Pritchard, *Theories of Primitive Religion* (O.U.P. 1965) for an account of psychological and sociological theories.

them. Scholars now tackle the question 'What is religion?' by trying to describe it rather than by trying to explain how it originated.

BELONGING

But what is the 'it' that is to be described? Is it a corporate activity, or is it a private matter between an individual and his Maker?

If we put the question in this way we have already revealed that we stand within a monotheistic tradition. The concept of a relationship between a man and his Maker would be meaningless in many other traditions. Some forms of Hinduism, for example, claim that there is no distinction between the eternal element in man (Ātman) and the reality that underlies the universe (Brahman); Ātman *is* Brahman. Then again, as we saw in Chapter 1, in Theravāda Buddhism questions about the gods are irrelevant to man's search for salvation. Even a form of Buddhism like the Japanese Pure Land school, which encourages its adherents to have a personal faith in a Buddha called Amida, would not apply the term 'maker' to him. And although many traditional religions, like those of Africa, believe in a supreme Being, the individual's relationship with him plays a very small part in the total pattern of the religion.

If we accept either of the two frequently quoted descriptions of religion: 'the flight of the alone to the Alone'[2] and 'what a man does with his solitariness',[3] we find that we have restricted ourselves to an even smaller part of mankind's religious map. This time we have left behind the other great monotheistic faiths such as Judaism and Islam. Individualism is very much a characteristic of our Western civilization. It developed within the European culture, and it found religious expression in certain strands of Christianity, particularly within Protestantism.

There is no religion in the world in which the individual is not considered to be important, either because he has to take responsibility for his own progress towards eventual liberation, as in Theravāda Buddhism, or because he is held responsible for carrying out regular observances, as in Islam and Judaism, or because, as in all religions, he has moral responsibilities.

[2] Plotinus.
[3] Alfred North Whitehead.

9

Religious experience (interpreted differently in different religions) is, of course, the experience of individuals. But this recognition of the significance of religion for the individual is not the same thing as saying that religion is a private matter. Belonging is an important element in religion. It may mean belonging to a small exclusive sect or to a faith whose adherents are numbered in hundreds of millions. It may mean being a member of an institution, like the Christian church or the Jewish synagogue, or of one of the organizations run by the church or the synagogue, like a youth group or a women's fellowship, or it may mean being a member of a tribe, where one's identity does not exist apart from the identity of the group. Whatever else we want to say about religion we cannot rule out the description of it as a corporate activity.

BELIEF

Perhaps we should rephrase our question and ask: Is religion about what people believe or about what they do? In the Christian tradition, especially in English-speaking countries, we have tended to concentrate on beliefs. Many discussions about religion centre on questions of belief. It is assumed that if a person believes that there is a God, he is religious, and if he doesn't, he is not. This emphasis on belief is not confined to the level of popular discussion and argument. Many books about religions written by academics have begun by giving an account of the religion's main beliefs and then only later, and in much less detail, have described its practices.

Why does belief play such an important part in Christianity? It is one of the very few religions in the world with credal statements, which set out the content of belief. Some Christian Churches include the recitation of a creed in their services of worship, and people who are being baptized or, in the case of babies, their sponsors, have to affirm certain beliefs. Christianity is one of the two major religions in which salvation is held to depend on what a man believes as well as on how he lives. The other is Islam, and it is not without significance that both of them developed out of existing religions. Because a new religion retains some of the elements of the religion out of which it emerges it becomes important to stress those aspects which are new and distinctive.

10

The official Christian statements of belief have come down to us in the form of creeds—the Apostles' and the Nicene—which were gradually hammered out on the anvil of controversy during the early centuries of the Church's history. By contrast, the content of Islamic belief is relatively brief and straightforward. A Muslim makes the affirmation, 'There is no God but God, and Muhammad is the Prophet of God', and he is required to believe in the unity of God, the existence of God's angels, the Book of God, God's Prophets, life after death, and the Day of Judgement.[4] This is partly because the beliefs which must be held by Muslims are laid down in the Qur'ān, and its form was fixed at a very early stage in the religion's development. For Muslims the Qur'ān contains, quite literally, the words of God, and its teachings are therefore not a matter for debate. The Christian scriptures, on the other hand, developed only slowly and in a piecemeal fashion. The Early Church had the Jewish Bible as its scriptures and although this gradually came to be called the 'Old Testament' as its own collection of writings grew, the canon of the New Testament was not finally closed until the fourth century A.D. The first Christians certainly did not regard the letters written by Paul and other church leaders, or even the gospels, as literally God's words. In addition, as the Christian faith spread from Palestine round the Mediterranean lands, its original Jewish form was modified as it was translated into the language and thought forms of the Greek-speaking world. The attempt to express exactly what the Christian faith meant or, rather, to say what it did *not* mean, was one of the reasons for the Church's concentration on matters of belief.

We have looked at the centrality of doctrine in Christianity to try to understand why a concentration on belief is such a common feature of Western definitions of religion, but that does not mean that belief is unimportant in other faiths. Every religion has a set of beliefs which together form a reasonably coherent system, and when we attempt to define religion, belief will be one of the aspects we must include.

It is worth asking, however, what part beliefs play in the life of the ordinary person, no matter how faithful an adherent of his religion he may be. Any systematic knowledge of beliefs tends to be confined to what might be described as the guardians and teachers of the faith, whether these are Jewish rabbis,

4 The Qur'ān, Sūra 4.136.

11

Muslim imāms, Hindu brahmins, the elders and the medicine men of traditional religions, or Taoist priests. This applies also to Christianity, in spite of the emphasis placed on belief. Christian ministers and theologians have been trained in theology, but the ordinary church member would find it difficult to give more than the vaguest outline of the major Christian doctrines, and rarer still would be the person who could explain the way in which doctrines are related to each other, e.g. Creation and the Work of Christ, or the Trinity and the Incarnation.

For the ordinary adherent beliefs tend to be a kind of back-cloth against which he practises his religion. There will be times when particular beliefs have special significance for him, but in the main they are not thought about in any systematic way. This does not mean that they are not important. They provide the framework of the religion, but they are expressed for the ordinary person through a variety of different aspects.

WORSHIP

They are expressed, for example, through worship or, in a religion like Theravāda Buddhism which does not have worship in the strict sense of the word, through meditation. It is not only the words that are used which express the beliefs, or even the way in which the pattern of worship is constructed—the sequence of different kinds of prayers, such as praise, confession, thanksgiving—or the use made of scriptures or other sacred stories; it is what is done as well as what is said.

Muslim worship provides an unusually clear illustration of beliefs expressed through action. *Salāt*, the regular prayers which the faithful Muslim says five times each day, involve a number of physical movements, including bowing and prostration—with the forehead on the ground. Each movement is related to the words it accompanies; through acts and words the worshipper offers praise and glory to God, and acknowledges his complete submission to God's will. At the end of the prayers each person acknowledges his relationship with his fellow men by turning his head first to the right and then to the left, saying each time 'Peace be on you, and the blessings of Allāh'. A similar belief is expressed by the custom of standing shoulder to shoulder. As the worshipper enters the mosque he joins those who are already standing in a straight line, facing in the direction of Mecca. The belief that all men are equal before God is shown by the fact that there is no distinction of rank; the humblest workman stands shoulder to shoulder with the most senior diplomat or the most influential businessman.

FESTIVALS

A religion's beliefs are also expressed through its festivals. In the annual cycle of festivals people are caught up in a recurring encounter with the religion's most fundamental beliefs. These beliefs are not presented in the form of systematic theology (though in monotheistic religions, and especially in Christianity, there may be accompanying expositions or sermons which spell out the doctrinal content of the festival); rather, they are presented in the form of stories, and the stories are frequently acted out or accompanied by traditional rituals of various kinds.

In the season of Lent, for example, Christians are reminded of the 'forty days and forty nights' of Jesus' temptation in the wilderness, and on the first day, Ash Wednesday, worshippers in some traditions have ash put on their foreheads to symbolize the repentance which is to characterize the period leading up to Easter. Another custom (observed by fewer Christians today than in the past) is the practice of some form of self-denial during Lent. Good Friday, the most solemn day in the Christian calendar, is marked by the reading of the account of Jesus' crucifixion, and by meditation on his words from the cross. In many churches the solemnity is shown by covering the cross with a black veil, and by the absence of flowers. Then on Easter Day churches are ablaze with light. The masses of white and yellow flowers and the candles and the white vestments worn by the clergy (in the Anglican, Roman Catholic and Orthodox branches of the Church) all 'speak' of new life as the worshippers hear again the story of the resurrection of Jesus.

Some festivals, like those which celebrate the renewal of nature in the spring or the gathering in of the harvest, acknowledge the power or powers which create and sustain life; some, like those which celebrate the birthday of the founder of the religion, remind the worshipper of the truths for which he stood, the light he brought into the world; some, like the Jewish Passover and the Christian Easter, re-present the events which were the foundation on which the faith was built. The most common theme, found almost universally, is the celebration of the triumph of good over evil, light over darkness.

It is probably true to say that there are no major beliefs in any religion which are not re-presented to its adherents, albeit in an indirect way, through the special occasions which make up its religious calendar.

RITES AND CUSTOMS

We have seen that rites and customs are usually associated with festivals, but their role in religion is much wider than that, and they deserve to be looked at separately. There are many ways in which beliefs are expressed by what people do, e.g. covering one's head or removing one's shoes in a place of worship, eating certain foods or abstaining from eating certain foods, either regularly or on special occasions; but the most important rituals are without doubt those which are known as the rites of passage. These are associated with the significant crises in man's life: birth, initiation, marriage, and death. Each of them marks the transition from one stage to another, a passing from the known to the unknown, an end as well as a beginning, and the elaborate ritual which accompanies them indicates this double aspect of threat and promise, not only to the actual persons involved but to the wider community.

In our society we have minimized the sharpness of the contrast between the stages before and after these occasions. When, for example, do young people feel that they have been initiated into adult life? Is it at puberty, or at the age when the law allows them to marry, or when they can be held legally responsible for their actions, or when they finish full-time education, or when they are confirmed or received into adult membership of a Church? Even the transition from life to death is less evident than it used to be. Death frequently takes place 'out of sight' of relatives and friends—and especially of children—and American funeral customs serve even more to blur the distinction between life and death.[5]

Judaism's way of handling the rites of passage is much more definite. The Bar Mitzvah ceremony, for example, when a boy reaches his thirteenth birthday, marks the break between child-

[5] See Evelyn Waugh, *The Loved One*. Penguin 1970.

hood and adult life in a completely unambiguous way. When he becomes a 'son of the commandment' a boy takes on the responsibility for observing the whole of the Jewish Law. He counts equally with the most respected elders in the community for making up a *minyan*—the number of adult male Jews needed for certain liturgical acts. In Orthodox synagogues, where men and women sit separately, he could, as a child, sit either with the men or with the women, but now he takes his place permanently with the rest of the men.

Judaism is equally unambiguous in its handling of death and burial. It has developed elaborate mourning rituals which are designed both to bring home the reality of death and to support those who have been bereaved by recognizing the need to express grief and then by helping them gradually to return to the routine of normal life.

It is in tribal communities, however, that we find the most vivid illustration of the importance of the rites of passage. Birth, initiation, marriage, and death are not only significant events in the life of the person involved or of his immediate family, they are significant for the whole community. They symbolize its life. For most African religions marriage is perhaps the central event because it symbolizes the continuity of the tribe, but they are all marked by careful and elaborate ritual in which the community participates, and which underlines the break with the past and the emergence into a new life. Initiation rites, which in most tribes take place at puberty, frequently include a dramatic enactment of death and rebirth, emphasizing the complete break with childhood and entry into adult membership of the society, with its knowledge, its status and its responsibilities. The initiate's education into everything that is involved in being an adult member of the community—hunting or agriculture or fishing, marriage, etc.—includes learning the traditional wisdom of the tribe, handed on from generation to generation in the form of myths, legends, proverbs, sayings, and so on. This brings us to another way in which a religion's beliefs are expressed.

SACRED TRADITIONS

Sacred writings (or the traditions which non-literate peoples hand on orally) are an important element in every religion. Some religions have two kinds of sacred literature: that which belongs

15

to the canon of the scriptures and that which is outside the canon but which is still regarded as authoritative. Examples of religions with these two kinds of sacred writings are: Hinduism, where the Vedas and the Upanishads are technically scriptures, but where the Bhagavad-Gītā and the Rāmāyana are for many millions of Hindus even more important; Judaism, which has the Talmud as well as the Bible; Islam, which has the Hadīths, or Traditions of the Prophet, as well as the Qur'ān; and Sikhism, which has the Dasm (Second) Granth as well as the Ādi (First) Granth.

Sacred writings are made up of very different types of literature, for example the Granth consists of hymns and prayers, the Rāmāyana is a mythological epic poem, the Qur'ān ranges from hymns of praise to detailed legislation for the functioning of the whole community, and the Jewish Bible (which is also the Christian Old Testament) is a whole library of books, containing sagas and prophecy, court chronicles and psalms, inscriptions and parables, laws and prayers.

In some religions sacred writings are used extensively in worship; in some the stories are a familiar part of the community's culture; in many they are associated with festivals and with the rites of passage. Traditional religions, as we have seen, frequently link the learning of the most sacred of the tribe's oral traditions with initiation into adult membership of the community. But whatever the role of sacred writings, and whatever their form, they help to mediate, directly or indirectly, a religion's beliefs to its adherents.

ETHICS

A religion's beliefs are also expressed through its code of ethics. Belief and action are closely related. The values which a religious community holds stem directly from its beliefs, and these values are translated into practice through the kinds of behaviour and, in some religions, the attitudes that lie behind the actual behaviour, which are expected of adherents. For example, what a community considers to be the right way to treat people springs from its beliefs about the nature of man and his place in the universe. In the Indian religious traditions all life is sacred, including the life of animals, because of the belief that it is possible for a man to be reborn as an animal. In monotheistic religions every individual is important because of the belief in a personal God who created and cares for every person.

Some religions include detailed prescriptions for behaviour in their sacred writings. This is particularly true of Judaism and Islam. In Buddhism the life and conduct of the monks is regulated by a section of the scriptures which is called the Vinaya Pitaka. In the Christian gospels ethical principles—like loving one's enemy, or 'going the second mile', or giving to Caesar what belongs to Caesar and to God what belongs to God—are more common than precise rules about how these principles are to be put into practice in actual situations. The Sikh scriptures, similarly, are concerned with moral principles rather than with specific actions.

In tribal communities, where a person's membership of the group is far more important than his existence as an individual, there are no conflicting codes of ethics. It is impossible to divide life into religious, social, political and personal aspects. They are all one. As young people grow up within the tribe they absorb this unified way of thinking and living. Even in secularized societies like ours, however, it is still possible to see the influence of the beliefs of the religion of the society on its laws and its generally accepted morality. Many people have consciously rejected both the Christian faith and its moral disciplines, yet the pattern of moral principles they want to affirm will usually be recognizably closer to that of Christianity than to that of other religions.

We have now looked at the different elements that go to make up 'religion'. We have seen that although an individual person's experience and response are important, religion also involves a corporate structure and organization. We have seen that although every religion has a coherent system of beliefs, for the ordinary person those beliefs will be expressed mainly through worship or meditation, festivals, rites and customs (especially the rites of passage), sacred writings and codes of ethics.

In recent years there have been a number of attempts to define what religion is in terms of its aspects, or dimensions. One such attempt was made by the British scholar, Ninian Smart. In his book *Secular Education and the Logic of Religion* (Faber 1968), pp. 15–18, Smart argues that religion is a 'complex object—a six-dimensional one', and he suggests that these six dimensions are doctrinal, mythological, ethical, ritual, experiential and

17

social.[6] Two American sociologists, C. Y. Glock and R. Stark, in their study of what is involved in being a religious person, suggest that five dimensions can be distinguished: experiential, ideological (beliefs), ritualistic, intellectual (knowledge about the basic tenets of the faith and its scriptures), and consequential (the implications for practical conduct). Glock and Stark's analysis is worked out in their book *Religion and Society in Tension* (Rand McNally 1965), ch. 2, but a similar account can be found in the extract from their later book, R. Stark and C. Y. Glock, 'American Piety: The Nature of Religious Commitment', included in *Sociology of Religion*, ed. Roland Robertson (Penguin 1969).

In the past there were a number of attempts to discover the 'essence' of religion, to isolate some experience, emotion or activity which could be said to belong only to the category 'religious' and to be common to all religions. There are two factors which made this a fruitless task. In the first place, increasing knowledge of other religions showed that there was such a wide diversity of beliefs and practices that it was not possible to find something which was common to all religions, and certainly not something which was regarded as equally important in all religions.[7] In the second place, as we have seen, religion is a complex affair. To concentrate on one activity, such as worship, is to ignore the fact that a religious person sees the whole of life in a religious perspective, and the rites and customs he observes, the festivals he celebrates, the code of ethics he follows, are no less aspects of his religion than worship is. We are likely to gain a more accurate understanding of the phenomenon of religion, therefore, if we recognize its complexity and take account of all its aspects.

[6] Smart's analysis can also be found in his book *The Religious Experience of Mankind* (Fontana 1971), ch. 1.

[7] The use of terms such as Hinduism, Buddhism and Christianity obscures the fact that within each religion there is a whole cluster of beliefs and practices. See further ch. 3.

18

3

STUDYING PARTICULAR RELIGIONS

The religious education class was learning about the Jewish Passover. Some of the pupils described how the Passover lambs were sacrificed in the Temple on the Day of Preparation, some did scale diagrams of the Temple, showing the different courts and the Temple building itself, some pretended that they were visiting Jerusalem for the festival for the first time and wrote a letter to a friend describing their experiences. Finally they mounted their work and put it up on the wall under the heading 'Jewish Festivals'.

A few weeks later they were studying Easter. This time they made a class newspaper. They read the stories in the gospels about the events in Jerusalem during Holy Week and tried to understand what it must have been like to be there. They wrote news items, feature articles, letters for the correspondence columns, and drew pictures of Jesus riding into Jerusalem on the first Palm Sunday, of him driving the money-changers out of the Court of the Gentiles in the Temple, and of the trial before Pilate.

In both cases these pupils were focusing on the first century C.E.[1] For the Jewish festival this meant the way it was celebrated at a particular stage in the history of the religion, at least six centuries after King Josiah of Judah made it one of the pilgrim festivals, for which people went to Jerusalem if they possibly could, and at least twelve centuries after it became one of the foundation festivals of the religion at the time of the Exodus. For the Christian festival on the other hand the pupils were studying the origin of Easter, the events which led up to the first Easter Day.

Does this matter? Does it matter, moreover, that these pupils were learning about a form of the Passover festival which ceased abruptly in 70 C.E.? For the Jews sacrifice could be offered to God only in the Temple in Jerusalem, and the sacrificing of the

[1] Common Era. See p. 34.

19

Passover lambs has therefore never been part of the festival since the destruction of the Temple in 70 C.E.

The illustration from this religious education syllabus raises the question: What is it that we should be focusing on when we study particular religions? The question can be raised in several ways. The example we have just used reminds us that religions change and develop. Even the Bahā'i faith, which is of comparatively recent origin, was founded over a hundred years ago, while Hinduism and Judaism go back for more than 3,000 years. Do we arbitrarily choose one particular period for our study? Does it matter if we select different stages in their development for different religions? Are we mainly interested in what a religion was like at some point in its past, or what it is like today?

Our study of any religion is going to be severely restricted if we answer any of these questions too rigidly. If we look at a religion only in the form in which it is found in the last quarter of the twentieth century we shall certainly mis-read at least some of its beliefs and practices, for these have been affected by a variety of factors belonging to its history. On the other hand, if we confine ourselves to the past we shall have a distorted understanding of the religion as a living faith today.

It has been characteristic of books written by Western authors to describe religions in a fairly 'academic' way, with accounts of their origins and their major beliefs, and perhaps their historical development, but with little indication of what it might be like to be an ordinary person, living out his daily life as an adherent of a religion, and with practically no mention of such an important aspect of a religion as its festivals.

A number of the books about world religions which have appeared in recent years, especially those designed for use in schools, have tried to redress the balance. But a strange thing has happened. They have presented religions like Hinduism and Islam as living faiths, giving us a much better insight into the life of a Hindu or a Muslim, but when they come to Christianity and Judaism some of them suddenly change their approach and concentrate almost entirely on the biblical period. This is a reflection both of the Christian (mainly Protestant) tradition of teaching about Christianity by recounting the biblical story, and of the largely unquestioned assumption that because

20

Christianity developed out of Judaism, Judaism virtually ceased with John the Baptist.

We shall return to some of these issues in later chapters. At the moment our primary concern is to draw attention to the kind of question we must consider when we set out to study particular religions.

SCHOOLS AND SECTS

Another question arises from the fact that a religion exists in a variety of forms. An exception has to be made in the case of primal religions, which are so inseparable from the total life of the tribe that it is virtually unthinkable that there should be splinter groups or dissident sects within the tribal community, but apart from this exception we find variations in belief and practice within all religions.

Islam is probably the most homogeneous of the major religions, but even Islam has a number of divisions within it. The Shī'as, for instance, consider that they are the true descendants of the original faith, rather than the Sunnis (the representatives of mainstream orthodoxy). Shi'ism developed within a few decades of Muhammad's death, not because of disagreement about doctrine or practice (though differences in these areas developed later) but because the Shī'as supported Ali, the fourth Caliph, who was Muhammad's son-in-law. The name Shī'a comes from a word which means 'to be a partisan of', and the partisans of Ali claimed that he was the only legitimate one of the four Caliphs who ruled the Islamic community in the period immediately after the Prophet's death, and that the caliphate belonged only to the house of Ali, who were also descendants of Muhammad through his daughter Fatima.

Disagreements about how a religious community should be governed have caused divisions in a number of religions, including Christianity, where, for example, the Independents (later the Congregationalists) separated themselves from the national Church. They claimed the right of each individual congregation, the 'gathered church', to appoint its own officials and to decide matters of belief and practice.

Divisions within religions have frequently resulted from different ways of interpreting the traditions they have inherited from the past. Catholic and Protestant strands in Christianity,

21

for example, have given different weight to the authority of the scriptures and of the historical Church in deciding doctrinal matters.

Perhaps the clearest illustration of this kind of division is to be found in Buddhism. Theravāda Buddhism claims that its teaching and practice go back to the Buddha himself. Mahāyāna Buddhism on the other hand claims that in the sixth century B.C., when Buddhism was founded, men were not able to apprehend all the truths which the Buddha had to teach, and that the later developments represent the gradual apprehension of these truths. Some of the later developments have moved so far from the original form of the religion that different schools of Buddhism can seem like different religions. For example, Theravāda Buddhists insist that the Buddha was a human figure who found enlightenment, and through his teachings showed others how they could obtain enlightenment, but one Mahāyāna school, the Japanese Pure Land sect (and the Chinese sect on which it was based) worships the Buddha Amida, and believes that salvation comes through faith in his name. Again, Theravāda Buddhists believe that it is not possible to attain nirvāna unless one *understands* the nature of man's predicament; the mind therefore plays an important part in achieving salvation. In complete contrast one of the Mahāyāna schools, Zen, believes that the mind is an obstacle to salvation; until man can break through the ordinary logical processes of reasoning he can never attain *satori*, enlightenment.

When groups within a religion are clearly differentiated from each other our task is reasonably straightforward. We have to recognize that what we learn about one section of a religion cannot be automatically taken to apply to the other sections; we have to be clear about which section or sections we are studying; and we have to treat with great wariness any book which uses such blanket expressions as 'Buddhists believe'.

IDEALS AND PRACTICES

Another form of the basic question we are considering in this chapter can be put like this: Do we study what a religion claims as its beliefs or do we study what its ordinary adherents actually believe? In no religion are the two identical. In Christianity, for example, there is a considerable difference between the

22

theologians' sophisticated interpretation of the doctrine of the Trinity and the understanding of it held by the 'man in the pew'. To start with, the word 'person' in the expression 'three persons in one God' originally referred to the mask which an actor wore to indicate to his audience the character he was portraying; today it suggests three separate persons, and much of the language of the Bible and of worship reinforces the idea that the Father and the Son are separate persons in the modern sense of the word. (See page 7.) We have said 'the Father and the Son' because most laymen are binitarian in practice, rather than trinitarian; the Holy Spirit is virtually ignored in popular Christian thinking.[2] The ordinary layman is not conscious of diverging from the classical doctrine of the Trinity; he might acknowledge his inability to understand the technical theology of his religion, but he would probably maintain with some definiteness that his beliefs were completely orthodox.

Human nature plays a part in another of the ways in which ideals and practices differ. Sikhism and Christianity, for example, both proclaim the breaking down of barriers within their faiths. Guru Nanak, the founder of Sikhism, rejected the caste system of Hinduism in which he had grown up, and declared that there must be no distinctions among his followers. But human inclination and social pressures make it difficult to maintain this ideal. In one suburb in London, for example, there are two gurdwaras (temples), one attended by the Sikhs who used to work on the land in their native Punjab, and the other by those who belong to higher castes.

The discrepancy between teaching and practice is even more marked in Christianity. Paul wrote, 'There is no such thing as Jew and Greek, slave and freeman, male and female; for all are one person in Christ Jesus' (Gal. 3.28), and James warned his readers that they should not treat the rich differently from the way they treated the poor (Jas. 2.1–7); yet there are still some parish churches in England with a special pew set aside for the squire and his family, and in several countries whose governments claim that they are preserving Christian values black Christians are not always welcome to share in the worship of 'white' churches, even within the same denomination.

If our study is confined to standard writings we shall meet

[2] The charismatic movements are doing something to redress the balance, at least as far as the gifts of the Spirit are concerned.

23

only the official teachings of a religion; if we encounter the living religion itself we may well come across considerable variations. Which is the real religion?

The gap between ideals and practices confronts us in a slightly different way in the syncretism which can be found in religions. In syncretism beliefs are drawn from two or more belief systems. It is not a new phenomenon in religion. It happened, for example, when the Israelites settled in Canaan. The prophets rebuked their contemporaries for mixing Canaanite Baal worship with the worship of the God of Israel. Hosea portrays the Lord as lamenting: 'When Israel was a boy, I loved him; I called my son out of Egypt; but the more I called the further they went from me; they must needs sacrifice to the Baalim and burn offerings before carved images.' (Hos. 11.1–2)

Sometimes syncretism is so pervasive that a totally new form of religion develops. This has been the case with some of the peoples of Latin America. They were converted to Christianity by their Spanish conquerors in the sixteenth century but they have interwoven with their Roman Catholicism many of their own Indian religious traditions.[3] More frequently syncretism takes the form of practices which are added to the original religion. Most religious developments in Japan have been of a syncretistic nature and it has been traditional, for example, for Buddhist priests to be asked to conduct funeral and memorial rites for adherents of Shinto or other faiths. Thailand provides another example. The official religion of the country is Theravāda Buddhism. This is the most austere form of Buddhism. It maintains that each man is responsible for his own salvation; it is by following the supreme Eight-fold Path of conduct, contemplation and wisdom that enlightenment can be attained. The Buddha discouraged any interest in gods or spirits as irrelevant to man's salvation. However, although this is the official teaching, many village homes have their small spirit shrines in the garden.

---

[3] This of course leads us into a different issue: how much is a people's identity bound up with its indigenous culture? In recent decades there has been a much greater awareness of the importance of cultural roots, and a number of attempts to restore a people's sense of dignity and self-respect have involved reviving and giving value to their culture. We have seen this, for example, with the Maori culture in New Zealand and the growth of black studies in the U.S.A.

Another question we have to ask is : Where does the boundary come between religion and life? We have already seen that this would be a meaningless question in tribal societies, but it is not without its problems in relation to the major historical religions. Jews and Muslims, for example, are insistent that there is no division between what is religious and what is non-religious. Obedience to God covers everything they do. There wasn't even a word for religion in the Hebrew language of the biblical period. In Orthodox Judaism today the way in which food is prepared the kinds of food which may or may not be eaten, and the way in which dishes are washed, are all as much an expression of a person's faith as the daily prayers or attendance at the synagogue. Islamic law covers every aspect of social as well as personal life, including such things as the laws of inheritance. Where then do we draw the line when we study religions such as these?

It is less difficult if we look at a religious community within an alien culture, for example, the Jewish or Muslim communities in Britain, but it is a much more complex issue if we consider the practice of Judaism in Israel or Islam in Pakistan or Indonesia. Muslims in particular would say that if Islam is to be truly practised it needs an Islamic state where law, education, government and social relationships can all be carried out according to God's will as revealed in the Qur'ān. The Five Pillars[4] are the foundation of Islam, and they can be practised in any situation, but Islam also consists of the whole superstructure designed to make it possible for a person to be *muslim*—obedient to God— in every aspect of life.

We have selected Judaism and Islam as examples of religions concerned with the whole of life. What about Christianity? Isn't it also concerned with the whole of life? This is certainly part of Christian teaching, but there has been a strange ambivalence in Christianity. The Christian doctrine of the Incarnation maintains that because—to use theological language—God became man, the whole of human life is sacred and there is therefore no barrier between the sacred (God's world) and the secular (not

[4] The Confession of faith (There is no God but God, and Muhammad is the Messenger of God); Prayer (five times a day); Almsgiving; Fasting during the month of Ramadan; Pilgrimage to Mecca.

25

God's world). Theology, however, does not exist in a vacuum, and a number of experiences have tended to make the distinction between sacred and secular a more dominant theme in the Christian tradition than the breaking down of the barrier between them.

In contrast to Islam, which existed as a political community governed by Muhammad from the time when he and his followers settled in Medina in A.D. 622, Christianity came into being in Palestine during a period when it was an occupied country. Until the beginning of the fourth century A.D., when the Roman Emperor Constantine was converted to Christianity, Christians were a powerless and often persecuted minority, and the contrast between what belonged to Caesar and what belonged to God was only too obvious. During and after the Reformation many Christian groups found themselves being persecuted for their beliefs, not by governments professing other religions but by governments of Christian countries. The puritan tradition, which flourished particularly in Britain and North America, distinguished sharply between what was 'of God' and what was 'of the world'. One of the legacies of this distinction is the current popular tendency to refuse the description 'religious' to anything which is not explicitly connected with God, Jesus, the Bible or the Church. In the debate about religious education some years ago many Christians even denied that such qualities as love, compassion and reconciliation were religious, declaring that to encourage such qualities in children was a merely humanist activity, inappropriate in religious education!

RELIGION AND CULTURE

A slightly different but highly significant form of the question about what constitutes a religion can be put like this: How do we draw a boundary around a religion? How, for instance, in our society do we distinguish what is Christianity from what is not? At the extremes of the spectrum this is not difficult. The celebration of Holy Communion is obviously Christian, witchcraft is just as obviously not. But where do we put Christmas? Christmas is a cultural festival, just as Divali and Holī are cultural festivals in India. One doesn't have to be a Christian to send Christmas cards or to cook a traditional Christmas dinner. Christmas has even been adopted as a popular children's festival in Japan.

Some Christians lament what they call the non-religious elements in Christmas. To them the only religious elements are theological and biblical—giving thanks to God for the gift of his Son, and retelling the nativity stories and the passages from the Old Testament which are considered to be looking forward to the birth of Jesus. But is it quite as straightforward as that? Christmas speaks to Christians of God's love to man, and in remembering his gift of his Son they remember the family into which Jesus of Nazareth was born. When in our society people take trouble to organize family reunions, when they celebrate Christmas with parties, when they are concerned with giving, when they make a special effort to bring happiness to those who live alone or to those who are in hospital, they are obviously acting in the spirit of Christmas. What criteria do we use to decide whether what they are doing is in any sense religious? Is it possible to put people who sing carols, or who listen to the service of lessons and carols on radio or television, into one of two clearly defined categories: religious and non-religious?

We might also ask: What about Santa Claus? Are the customs associated with him Christian? The name comes from St Nicholas, a fourth-century bishop of Myra, and the customs linked with Santa Claus recall his acts of generous and anonymous giving.

Christmas is certainly a Christian festival. It is also a folk festival. When we are studying the Christian religion, therefore, how much of it do we include? Is it right to exclude any part of it?

Folk religion plays an important part in every society. Many people, for example, turn to the Christian Church only for the rites of passage—ceremonies connected with birth, marriage and death. What is our attitude to those who feel that it would be wrong not to have the baby 'done'? Do we dismiss them as superstitious? Or do we see in their concern a dimly apprehended belief that there is more to life than material values? Many couples who have no overt Christian belief choose to be married in a church. Is it only because of the setting? Would they be equally happy if they were allowed to have the photos taken in the church porch after a registry office wedding?

Still using marriage as an example we can ask another question about boundaries. Is Christian marriage only the service of worship in the church and the vows taken before God? Does it

27

include symbols like the ring? What about a symbol of luck like a horseshoe, with its original associations with moon worship and the use of iron as a protection against magic? Does a pagan symbol become 'Christian' when it is used by Christians, or does it remain for ever a pagan intrusion into Christianity?

Distinguishing between a religion and its culture may be difficult in any religion; it is particularly difficult in Hinduism. The very word 'Hinduism' as the name of a religion was a foreign invention. The word 'Hindu' simply means 'Indian', and millions of Indians would be astonished to be told that they belonged to the Hindu religion. Indeed, there is no such thing as *the* Hindu religion. A complex religious pattern has developed on the Indian sub-continent over the past three to four millennia, and virtually the whole spectrum of religious beliefs and practices can be found under its umbrella. (See pages 57f.)

Popular books about Hinduism used to say that it was a social system rather than a religion. This was misleading because readers who were used to distinguishing rather sharply between religion and society gained the impression that it was merely a system for ordering people's 'secular' relationships. It has come as a surprise to many Westerners to discover the rich religious life of ordinary Hindu people. There is, however, an important truth in the popular description. Hinduism is a whole way of life, and there is no absolute dividing line between a person's 'religious' activities and his 'social' activities.

An interesting idea has been put forward by the American scholar, Wilfred Cantwell Smith. He has suggested that the word 'religion' is so ambiguous that we should stop using it. The word 'religions' he finds even less helpful. He points out that giving a name to a religion is a comparatively recent phenomenon. There are occasional occurrences as far back as the Renaissance but we owe the custom of referring to religions as Buddhism, Hinduism, Confucianism, etc., mainly to the nineteenth century.

In place of the word 'religion' he would put two expressions, 'cumulative tradition' and 'personal faith'. Traditions are made up of all the beliefs, customs, formularies, sacred writings, which have come down to us from the past. They are what we see when we look at a particular religion. Traditions will be different in different countries and within different sections of the same religion, and they are inseparable from their cultural context.

28

Faith on the other hand is the individual person's response to the transcendent, whether he understands this in terms of a personal God or in some other way.[5]

Wilfred Cantwell Smith's ideas have not gone unchallenged. The debate will be carried on by those involved in the study of religions, but in the meantime his suggestion serves as a useful reminder to us that when we undertake the study of particular religions we have no neat, clear-cut boundaries to define the object of our study.

[5] See *The Meaning and End of Religion.* Mentor 1964.

Part 2

QUESTIONS OF UNDERSTANDING

4

GETTING IT RIGHT

What you do not like if done to yourself, do not do to others.
What is hateful to yourself do to no other.
Always treat others as you would like them to treat you.

These three examples of the Golden Rule come from the teachings of Confucius, the Chinese sage who lived in the sixth century B.C., from Hillel, the Jewish rabbi who was a contemporary of Jesus, and from Jesus himself. The insistence that one should treat others as one would wish to be treated oneself is included in the ethical precepts of most human communities, and we cannot do better than apply it to our study of other people's religions.

First and most important, we have to recognize that when we study a living religion we are concerned not merely with an academic set of facts about beliefs and practices, but with the faith of men, not merely with religions called Judaism or Hinduism, but with the faith of Jews or Hindus. As Max Warren has said: 'Our first task in approaching another people, another culture, another religion, is to take off our shoes, for the place we are approaching is holy. Else we may find ourselves treading on men's dreams.'[1]

One of the ways in which we treat another person's religion with respect is to aim always at accuracy. In one sense the whole of this book is about 'getting it right', but in this chapter we are going to look specifically at some of the basic ways in which the Golden Rule can be put into practice.

SPELLING

We start with something which may seem trivial but which can easily be a cause of confusion. In our study we shall meet words

[1] General introduction to the *Christian Presence* series, S.C.M. Press.

31

from other languages. Most of these languages have different scripts from ours, and different 'alphabets'. Hebrew, for example, has twenty-two consonants. Two of them are slight variants of our *t* sound, and another two are slight variants of our *s*, but there is no equivalent of the English sound *j*. Conversely, there is no English equivalent of the Hebrew guttural ע (*'ayin*).

Words from languages with different scripts have to be transliterated, that is, they are written with letters from our alphabet, with the aim of indicating how the words are pronounced in the original language. It would be relatively simple if there were a standard system of transliteration for each language, but unfortunately there is not. This can be illustrated with a familiar example from Hebrew. The letter י can be transliterated as either *y* or *j*, and the letter ו as either *w* or *v*, which is why we find the divine name—יהוה—in books about the Old Testament written as Jahweh or Yahweh or Jahveh or Yahveh.

Similarly, when we read books about Islam we may find three of the most important words in the religion written either as Mohammed, Moslem and Korān or as Muhammad, Muslim and Qur'ān.[2] The second group is actually a better transliteration because it approximates more closely to the Arabic original. It is being used increasingly in preference to the anglicized transliteration of the first group, and it is sensible for us to use it too.

Many standard books on religions give a brief explanation of the system they have adopted. R. C. Zaehner's *Hinduism*, for example, is prefaced by a 'Note on Transliteration and Pronunciation'.

Diacritical marks are another aid to pronunciation. These are the distinguishing marks attached to letters, as in Bhagavad-Gītā, *jñāna*, Ṛg-Veda. Most scholarly works include them but popular books leave them out on the assumption that ordinary people would not want to be bothered with them. This may apply to the complete range of diacritical marks but it could be argued that 'ordinary people' are the readers most in need of the marks which help with pronunciation. It is helpful, for instance, to have long vowels marked. This applies especially in the case of the languages used in the Indian religious traditions. Not only do they tend to have a large number of long words which can be quite daunting when we meet them for the first time, but the

---

[2] The *u* is pronounced as in *put* and not as in *cut*.

syllables on which the stress falls are frequently not those which we would naturally have chosen. For example, English people tend to pronounce Mahāyāna[3] as if it were Māhayāna, and Rāmānuja (a Hindu scholar who lived in the eleventh century A.D.) as if it were Rāmanūja. When the long syllables are marked we can even pronounce with some confidence the name of the Hindu epic, the Mahābhārata (pronounced as if it were Ma-hāb-hā-ra-ta). If we make a point of always marking the long vowels in our own writing we shall find that the correct pronunciation of the more frequently used words soon becomes second nature to us.

Slightly more difficult are the Sanskrit sounds which are usually transliterated as ṛ and ś and ṣ. Without knowing that ṛ represents the sound ri we might think that the word smṛti was unpronounceable. For this reason some authors transliterate the Sanskrit word as smriti.[4] Similarly with ś and ṣ which are both pronounced sh. The names of the gods Śiva and Viṣnu, for example, are often written as Shiva and Vishnu.

Quite apart from the question of pronunciation, this kind of knowledge alerts us to the fact that we may have to look in more than one place in an index or a glossary to find a particular word.

Another kind of variation occurs when a word is pronounced differently today from the way it was pronounced in the past. The Hebrew consonant ת (tau), for example, used to carry the sound th as in 'both' when it came at the end of a word, but in modern Hebrew it has become a hard t, so we may find the word for unleavened bread transliterated as matzoth or as matzot (or mazzoth or mazzot) and the word for tabernacles or booths as succoth or succot (or sukkoth or sukkot). This is further complicated by the practice in some places of reducing the final t to s; in American books, for example, we frequently find variations like matzos and sukkos—and Shabbos for Shabbat, Sabbath.

We turn to Buddhism for our last illustration of possible confusion over spelling. Theravāda Buddhism uses Pali for its writings, while much of the Mahāyāna literature is in Sanskrit. As a result we find both the Pali forms, like nibbāna, dhamma,

---

[3] The short a is pronounced like the a in China.

[4] Smriti means 'remembered'. It is the word used for one of the two categories of Hindu sacred writings. (See p. 59.)

and *kamma*, and their Sanskrit counterparts, *nirvāna*, *dharma*, and *karma*. Some Buddhist words, including these three, have entered the English language in their Sanskrit form, so it is not easy to be rigorous about using the Pali form when we are dealing with Theravāda Buddhism.

CHOOSING OUR WORDS

In Chapter 5 we shall be looking at the problems involved in trying to understand the meaning conveyed by words and expressions from other cultures. At this stage we are concerned with the rather more manageable task of choosing the right vocabulary.

If we apply the Golden Rule in this area we shall be careful to avoid using words or expressions which the adherents of a religion find offensive. For example, Muslims object to their religion being called Muhammadanism. They worship God, not Muhammad, who was only the Messenger of God. The name Islam, meaning 'submission to God', describes the religion more accurately.

We shall also avoid using the name Old Testament when we are referring to the Jewish Bible. Old Testament is the right name to use for exactly the same body of literature when we are talking about the Christian Bible because it indicates Christianity's belief that in Jesus Christ God made a new covenant with his people, and the story of this covenant is contained in the 'New Testament'.[5] For Judaism, however, its scriptures contain the story of *the* covenant, and the suggestion that it has been superseded would be completely unacceptable.

It is equally easy to see why the use of B.C. and A.D. is inappropriate for Judaism. Not only does it involve the acknowledgement of Jesus as the turning point in history, but Anno Domini means 'in the year of our Lord', an affirmation of the theological significance of Jesus. The convention, therefore, has grown up of using B.C.E. and C.E. ('Before the Common Era' and 'Common Era') for writings which are not internal to the religions.

[5] The Greek word for covenant, *diathēkē,* appeared in the Latin translations as *testamentum,* and so came into English as 'testament'.

Words which have acquired negative associations are best avoided, even when a term is a technically accurate one, as in the case of 'primitive'. In anthropology a primitive society is one that has relatively simple structures in contrast to the highly differentiated structures and specialized roles of 'civilized' societies. However, we have imported a value judgement into the terms. We assume that the more civilized people are, the better they are, so the word 'primitive' has come to have associations of inferiority. It also suggests a very early stage of development, and so we contrast 'primitive' and 'advanced'. We take it for granted, of course, that we belong in the categories 'civilized' and 'advanced' when the words are used in their value-bearing sense as well as when they are used in their technical sense! Words which have been used in an attempt to avoid the unfortunate connotations of 'primitive' are 'primal', 'tribal' and 'traditional'. Anthropologists also use 'small scale' and 'face-to-face', but these terms are descriptions of societies and cannot be applied in the same way to religions.

Another word with negative associations is 'idol'. Christian hymnology has reinforced the idea that men actually worship the images of their gods. 'The heathen[6] in his blindness bows down to wood and stone', we used to sing in Bishop Heber's missionary hymn, 'From Greenland's icy mountains'. We described it as idolatry, because idolatry means putting something in the place of God and giving it the worship due to God. Muslims frequently accuse Hinduism of idolatry, making the same assumption that because the gods are represented in the form of images Hindus are worshipping the images. Hindus refute this charge indignantly. For them an image is not the God. It symbolizes the God who is the object of their worship. Similarly, tribal peoples believe that a god or a spirit can be present in an image or in a natural object such as a tree or a mountain, but it is to the god or the spirit that they make their offering, not to the object itself.

Sometimes an unfortunate impression can be given by the English word which is used to translate a word from its original language. This has happened in the case of the Arabic word *hijra* (or *hijrah*). *Hijra* means literally 'emigration'. It is used of

[6] 'Heathen' is another pejorative word, and so is 'pagan' when it is not used in a technical sense.

35

Muhammad's move from Mecca to Medina in A.D. 622 (1 A.H.[7]). The traditional English translation—'flight'—could be thought to imply that Muhammad was running away from Mecca, so the word 'migration' is now more widely used.

A misleading impression of a different kind is given by the translation of the Pali word *ārya* as 'noble'. We meet it particularly in Buddhism's 'Four Noble Truths' and 'Noble Eightfold Path'. In one sense it is an accurate translation, because the idea of nobility is included in the meaning of *ārya*, but the English word 'noble' implies that something is excellent, high-ranking; it does not necessarily mean that nothing ranks higher. For Buddhists, however, the Four Noble Truths are not merely ideas which are worthy of admiration; they provide the diagnosis of man's condition and the remedy for it. Sometimes the word 'supreme' is used instead of 'noble'; it comes nearer to suggesting that the Four Truths are concerned with ultimate reality, with what Buddhists believe to be *the* truth about human life. The word 'noble', however, has become so firmly established that it may not be possible now to replace it.

There are two other expressions which it is probably too late to change, though they are both offensive to adherents of other religions. One is the association of the name Mecca with ballroom dancing. It is easy to see why the name was thought to be appropriate. Mecca is the most important city in the world for Muslims, who try to make the pilgrimage to it at least once in their life-time. It is therefore a place to which all eyes turn, a place which attracts vast numbers of people. Mecca dance-halls, however, have nothing else in common with Islam's sacred city. Even more offensive to Muslims, who have strict views about women being modestly dressed, is the fact that the Miss World beauty competition is sponsored by a company that calls itself Mecca Limited.

The other expression which is firmly established in the English language is 'pharisaical'. Its meaning is given in the dictionary as 'The character and spirit of the Pharisees; hypocrisy; formalism; self-righteousness', so it is hardly surprising that Jews find it offensive. Because the gospels include a number of conflict stories in which Jesus is portrayed as being critical of the Pharisees, Christians came to the conclusion that all Pharisees were legalistic hypocrites. There are actually some passages in

[7] The first year of the Muslim era. A.H. stands for Anno Hijra.

the gospels which show the Pharisees in a better light,[8] but these seem to have gone unnoticed, and it has been comparatively recently that Christians have realized how great was Pharisaism's contribution to the positive development of Judaism. They have been surprised to discover that the Pharisees themselves were not uncritical of those of their members who treated the Law as an end in itself instead of as a means to an end. The Pharisees' own classification of the seven different kinds of Pharisee gives us an interesting glimpse into their thinking—and their sense of humour.

The shoulder Pharisee—who parades his virtue.

The 'wait-a-little' Pharisee—who temporizes.

The bruised Pharisee—who bangs into a wall in his anxiety to avoid looking at a woman.

The pestle Pharisee—with his head bowed down in mock humility.

The reckoning Pharisee—calculating his virtues.

The God-fearing Pharisee.

The God-loving Pharisee.

Only the last two are commended.

SOURCES

The stereotype which Christians have had of the Pharisees leads us naturally to another area in which it is important to apply the Golden Rule. None of us would be happy if the main source of information about Christianity was the writings of people who were antagonistic towards it. Yet this is how Judaism has for centuries been treated by all but a minority of Christians. In recent years, however, there has been increasing awareness of how much we have missed in our understanding of Judaism by ignoring Jewish scholarship.

It would be quite wrong to suggest that only books written by adherents of a religion could be trusted. There is a large number of able scholars who are recognized authorities on different aspects of the study of religions. One of the things we have to do is to build up gradually our knowledge of who the authorities are in the area of our study. It is in their books that

[8] E.g. the stories of Nicodemus (John 3.1f.) and of the scribe—who would have been a Pharisaic scribe—who was praised by Jesus (Luke 10.25–8).

we are likely to find the most thorough treatment of the subject, and they provide a reliable guide when we find apparently contradictory statements in two or more of our sources.

We should, however, always use some of the literature which comes from the religion we are studying. This could be of several different kinds.[9] We shall take our illustrations from Judaism.

Apart from sacred writings, which we shall come back to, the first kind is the standard work of scholarship which is known internationally (e.g. Jacob Neusner, ed., *Understanding Rabbinic Theology*, Ktav Publishing House 1974). Then there is the study intended for a more general readership (e.g. Alfred Jospe, ed., *Tradition and Contemporary Experience*, Schocken 1970). Some books are written in order to explain the religion to outsiders (e.g. Herman Wouk, *This is my God*, Collins 1973, first published 1959, a readable personal description; Lionel Blue, *To Heaven with Scribes and Pharisees*, Darton, Longman and Todd 1975, a book which conveys the 'feel' of Judaism; A. I. Polack and J. Lawrence, *Cup of Life*, S.P.C.K. 1976, the history of Judaism from biblical times). Others are written for the adherents of the religion,[10] and these can often give us a real insight into what it is like to belong to the faith (e.g. Maurice Lamm, *The Jewish Way in Death and Mourning*, Jonathan David 1969, a book which provides detailed information as a guide to Jews who may not be as rigorous in their observance as their more orthodox brethren). Books written for children and young people are particularly useful. Not only do they give us valuable insight into the way in which children are nurtured within the religious tradition but, because they are explaining the beliefs and practices in a simple, introductory way, they enable us to understand them more easily (e.g. Morris Epstein, *All about Jewish Holidays and Customs*, Ktav Publishing House 1959).

We return now to the sacred writings and other texts of a more permanent nature. Under the last heading come forms of worship, prescribed ritual, etc. (e.g. the Haggadah, used for the Passover meal; S. Singer, tr., *The Authorised Daily Prayer Book*,

[9] The distinctions must not be treated too rigidly; many books fall into more than one of the categories.

[10] It is seldom possible to obtain these books from ordinary bookshops, but the main religious traditions in a country will have outlets for their publications.

Eyre and Spottiswoode, which contains, in addition to the order of worship for synagogue services, prayers for Bar Mitzvah, weddings, funerals, the festivals, etc., grace before and after meals, and even children's morning and evening prayers). There is, however, the danger that we might think of worship being offered only in the form of set prayers, so we should also look at books of prayers for more informal use (e.g. A. J. Goldman, tr., *Blessed art Thou*, Hebrew Publishing Company, N.Y. 1961; *Prayers and Blessings*, Religious Art Production, for young children).

A religion's sacred writings are the most important of our primary sources. These will include the scriptures and, for many religions, writings which are regarded as authoritative even though they are not technically scriptures (e.g. the Talmud. A. Cohen, *Everyman's Talmud*, Dent, is a summary of the teaching of the Talmud, but H. Danby, *The Mishnah*, O.U.P., is a translation of the Mishnah, which is part of the Talmud. One of the sections of the Mishnah, 'Ethics of the Fathers', can be found in the *Authorised Daily Prayer Book*).

Most sacred writings are lengthy and we need help in finding our way round them. In the case of anthologies it is preferable to use those which have been compiled by an adherent of the religion or by a scholar who is a recognized authority on the religion. We have to remember that sacred writings are always interpreted writings. They belong within the religion and they cannot be understood properly apart from it. We must therefore be careful not to jump to conclusions about a religion's beliefs on the basis of isolated passages. (See further pages 59f.)

If we want to understand a religion we have to ask what a particular belief or practice, story or event, means to a believer, not what it means to us, and what better way is there to supplement our study of literature than by getting to know adherents of the religion? If we are fortunate enough to live in a town or city where there are other religious communities this is fairly straightforward. Most communities welcome contact with people who are genuinely anxious to find out about their faith, and it is usually possible to attend their places of worship. To have personal friends who are adherents of another religion is even better. Religions are *lived*. Some, like Hinduism and Judaism, are centred mainly on the home, and it is when we see a religion being practised that it can really begin to come to life for us.

We must beware, however, of generalizing from particular experiences. We may get to know members of one particular sect without realizing that they are not representative of the religion as a whole. We may encounter customs which are characteristic of a particular region or of a particular country— or even of a particular family. One Jewish woman commented that she was sure her small children thought that apple crumble was a traditional Sabbath dish, like chicken soup and gefilte fish, but the reason they had it so frequently for the special Friday evening meal was because it was her husband's favourite pudding!

It may be thought that the suggestions outlined above are wildly idealistic. Is it really necessary to go to such lengths? Why not just use the popular books which have been written for the very purpose of informing their readers about world religions? Perhaps we should turn the question round the other way and ask what advice we would give to someone from another religion who wanted to learn about Christianity. What aspects would we want him to include in his study? The life of Jesus, and the beginnings of the Christian Church? What about the Old Testament? The creeds? The Reformation? The Church today? But which Church? Roman Catholic, Eastern Orthodox, Anglican, Methodist...? The charismatic movements? The ecumenical movement? The missionary expansion of the Church? Christian ethics? Intercessory prayer? Liturgical worship? Church architecture? Christian symbolism? Christianity and science? Church and society? Christian Aid and Tear Fund? The ministry? Synods and assemblies? Monastic orders? The attributes of God? Doctrines of the Trinity, the Incarnation, the Atonement...? The problem of evil? The sacraments? Christmas, Easter, Pentecost? Harvest festivals?

How many items of this random—and incomplete—list could be included in a book which covered several world religions? How accurate would the reader's understanding be if each of these topics were dealt with in a few sentences, or even a few paragraphs? If we are to treat other men's religions as we would want them to treat ours we shall aim at the most thorough understanding possible—and we shall know that even then we have only begun on a journey of exploration which can continue through a life-time.

5

WORLDS APART

'Transculturalization' is a comparatively new word which has
been widely used in recent years. We may not like the sound
of it but its meaning is important in an age when we have
become increasingly aware of other peoples and their distinctive way of life. It means making a transfer from one culture
to another. As we saw in Chapters 2 and 3, religions are em-
bedded in cultures, and to study another religion means to enter
a completely different world.

This is not a new problem for Christians, whose religion took
its origin in the Middle East. The first Christians were Jews,
and they naturally interpreted their experience in the language
and thought forms of their Hebraic culture. As the faith spread
into the Graeco-Roman world, so it was expressed in ways
which could be understood by men of a quite different culture.
In fact Christianity, more than any other religion except
Buddhism, bears the marks of its encounter with other cultures
as it has been carried round the world from one country to
another. Much of what we think of as 'Christian' is the impress
of our European culture on a religion of Semitic origin. In the
nineteenth century peoples in many parts of the world who came
into contact with Christian missionaries thought that such things
as Western-style church architecture and furnishings, and even
English hymn tunes, were an integral part of the Christian faith.

In this chapter we shall look at three of the areas in which we
have to make a particular effort to step out of our own world
and see things from the perspective of a different world if we
are to understand the concepts of other religions.

WORDS

The first area is language. How can we convey the actual
meaning of words for which there is no exact equivalent in
another language? This is a perennial problem for translators.

41

How, for instance, should the Welsh word *hiraeth* be translated? English words like 'longing', 'yearning', even 'homesickness', can give some indication, but none of them is capable of conveying the depth of meaning which *hiraeth* holds for the Welsh.

The work of translating the Bible is particularly fraught with difficulties. How, for example, should the Hebrew word *hesed*[1] be translated? It is the key word in the prophet Hosea's plea to Israel to be faithful in keeping her side of the covenant relationship with God. The translators of the King James Bible employed three different English words for *hesed*: loving-kindness, goodness and mercy. Admittedly these translators used a variety of English words on principle (which is one of the reasons why the English of the Authorized Version is noted more for its beauty than for its accuracy), but in this case none of the three words conveys to us what the word *hesed* would have conveyed to its original hearers—faithfulness within a covenant relationship. Among modern translations the Revised Standard Version has love, steadfast love and kindness, the New English Bible loyalty, unfailing devotion and mutual trust, and the Jerusalem Bible love, tenderness and kindness.

More misleading, however, is the use of words which have a similar but not identical meaning, like the use of 'incarnation' for the Sanskrit word *avatāra*. *Avatāra* means literally 'descent'. Vaishnavite Hindus, who worship Vishnu as the supreme God, believe that in times of extreme wickedness Vishnu descends to this world for the purpose of destroying evil. Vishnu's eighth *avatāra*, Krishna, features in the Bhagavad-Gītā. In the poem Krishna, acting as the charioteer of the warrior Arjuna, explains to Arjuna the nature of man and the paths that lead to salvation. It will already be obvious that the concept of incarnation in Hinduism is not identical with the concept of incarnation in Christianity, in spite of some similarity. Vaishnavites believe that there have been a number of *avatāras* of Vishnu, in forms such as those of a fish and a boar as well as in human form. But even the *avatāras* in human form, like those of Rāma and Krishna, were not fully human. They appeared as men but they were not constrained by human limitations of knowledge or power. In Hinduism God visits man to rescue him; he is not identified with man. 'Incarnation' may be the nearest that we

[1] Also transliterated *chesed* and *hesed*. The first consonant is a guttural, pronounced rather like the *ch* in the Scottish word 'loch'.

42

can get in English, but it would be wrong to transfer to its use in Hinduism our understanding of it in Christianity.

The translation of the Hebrew *torah* by the word 'law' creates a similar problem. Of course Torah does mean law, but it has a more positive and a more comprehensive meaning in Judaism than it does in normal English usage. We tend to think of laws as restrictive. I am not allowed by law to drive my car above a certain speed on the public highway. I am not allowed by law to build a house in any area not scheduled for development. We talk about 'falling foul of the law'. To the observant Jew, however, the Law is not a burden; it is a joy. He can say with the Psalmist, 'O how I love thy Law!' (Ps. 119.97), and it is not without significance that the Jewish compilers of the Psalter felt it appropriate to preface the whole collection with a psalm in praise of the Law. In Judaism the Law is the Law of the Lord, and to observe the Law is to be faithful to God. Christians who accuse Judaism of being legalistic have not understood the concept of Torah. To a Jew Torah is the revealed will of God. Its basic expression is found in the first five books of the Bible, which are therefore called the Torah, but it covers every aspect of life. Sometimes Torah is translated as 'teaching', but there is no single English word which adequately conveys its meaning.

Similarly there is no English word which conveys the meaning of one of the key words in Hinduism and Buddhism: *dharma* (Pali: *dhamma*). The entry on the Buddhist usage in *A Dictionary of Comparative Religion*[2] says that it is translated into English variously as 'religion, truth, doctrine, righteousness, virtue, essence, elemental ultimate constituent or "atom", phenomena, law, norm, property, and entity'. The word most commonly used in the books we are likely to be consulting is 'teaching' (surprisingly omitted from the above list, though mentioned later in the same article). The Sanskrit root from which the word is derived means 'to support', and the Dharma of the Buddha—his teachings—provide the support or foundation for a righteous life, that is, the right kind of life. The Buddha's Dharma is also called his doctrine. It is more than a set of ethical precepts; it is a system of beliefs about the nature of man's condition as well as guidance about the way man should live if he is to attain nirvāna.

[2] S. G. F. Brandon, ed., Weidenfeld and Nicolson 1970.

The Hindu concept of *dharma* is slightly different from that of Buddhism. It is the nearest that Hinduism gets to a word for religion. It means law, or sacred law, but in the sense of an ordered situation. Vaishnavites believe that when Vishnu's *avatāras* destroy evil they restore *dharma* to the world. Eternal Dharma, the sacred law of the universe, should be reflected in *dharma* in human society. Man's *dharma* is to do his duty according to the position in which he finds himself in life. In the Bhagavad-Gītā it is Arjuna's duty to fight because he is a Kshatriya, a member of the warrior caste. But 'law', 'order', 'duty' are far too restricted in their meaning to do justice to the concept of *dharma* in Hinduism.

We have looked at a very small number of examples, but enough to show something of the problems of conveying the meaning of the concepts of a religion to someone from a different culture.

IMAGERY

A religion's cultural context is relevant in a different way when we come to its use of imagery—metaphor, simile, analogy, symbolism, etc. Even climate can make a difference. The idea of a cloud as an image conveys little to people who live in a country with a high average rainfall. To the biblical writers and their readers, who experienced every year at least five months with no rain, and who knew that in some years the rains would not come at all, the appearance of the first clouds after the dry season was a sign of life and hope. For them there was an intensity and depth of meaning in the use of 'cloud' to represent the glory and the presence of God.

The word 'image' means likeness, and imagery is of necessity employed when men wish to speak of something which transcends their experience. This applies, for instance, in 'descriptions' of life after death. Even here cultural factors, including geography, influence the choice of images. Islam originated in the desert lands of the Arabian peninsula; the Arabic word normally translated 'paradise' means 'the garden', and flowing water is a common feature of Muslim descriptions of paradise.[3]

Gehenna, the Aramaic word which came to be used for hell

[3] The word 'paradise' comes from the Persian word for a nobleman's garden.

44

in late biblical Judaism, and which is found also in the New Testament as 'hell' or 'fires of hell', owes its origin to a city rubbish dump. The valley of Hinnom (Hebrew: *Gē Hinnom*), outside the south wall of the city of Jerusalem, was turned into a rubbish dump by King Josiah in the seventh century B.C.E. in his attempt to desecrate a place which had been used for sacrifices made to 'heathen' gods. The continually smouldering refuse dump gave to the idea of a place of punishment after this life the images of the fire that is not quenched and the devouring worm that never dies (cf. Mark 9.48).

Imagery may occur in verbal form or it may be expressed visually. In Hinduism, for example, iconography is particularly important. To ignore the pictorial representation of its abundant mythology and its gods is to ignore a significant aspect of the religion.

Imagery is never meant to be taken literally. It points beyond itself to a deeper level of meaning. The first level of meaning of some images is relatively easy for us to grasp once it has been explained to us. We don't need to have seen a lotus, the Buddhist symbol of purity, to be able to visualize its flower rising pure and unstained from the muddy waters in which it is growing. To penetrate to the second level of meaning, however, requires a considerable knowledge of the religion. In Buddhism, for example, the purity which the lotus symbolizes is more than just moral purity; it is non-attachment, freedom from craving of any kind, and we are likely to get a misleading impression of what this means to a Buddhist unless we can set it in the context of his belief about the goal of man's life.

To Westerners the many-armed figures of Hindu iconography may seem strange. When we are told that many arms symbolize many attributes we have reached the first level of understanding, but a much greater familiarity with Hindu mythology is needed before we can come anywhere near grasping the significance of the conch shell, the discus, the mace and the lotus which the God Vishnu carries, or the jewel and curled mark on his breast, or the dark blue colour of his skin. The imagery associated with the God Shiva is even more complex because in Hindu thinking he is the reconciliation of all opposites. He may therefore be represented as the great ascetic, a naked yogi smeared with ashes, rapt in silent contemplation in the fastnesses of the Himalayas, with a third eye and a crescent moon in the middle

45

of his forehead and the sacred river Ganges flowing from his matted hair. Or he may be shown as the four-armed Lord of the dance, surrounded by a circle of flames, performing the dance of cosmic joy, dancing creation into existence. Or as Bhairava, the terrible destroyer, whose frenzied dance represents the destruction of the world at the end of the *kalpa*.[4] Or as the Lord of the beasts, with the character of a fertility god. In the Hindu cyclic concept of time, destruction implies reproduction, and it is under the emblem of the *lingam*, or phallus-shaped pillar, that Shiva is worshipped as the supreme Being by the sects that bear his name, the Shaivites. In this paragraph we have only touched the fringe of Hindu imagery; it would be a rash person who claimed to understand Hinduism on the basis of having read a couple of books about the religion!

A religion's imagery is not static. Some images of course have remained powerful for centuries, and even for millennia, but men also use the images of their own period to express the beliefs which have been handed down to them. Christian hymns of the Victorian period describe heaven in terms of heavenly choirs and the playing of harps, but one of the most interesting images favoured by this industrial society with its doctrine that work was a virtue is the concept of rest as an appropriate image of bliss in the next life. One hymn writer whose piety was greater than his knowledge of children's ideas of pleasure even suggested that there would be a 'rest for little children above the bright blue sky'.

The significance of imagery can change with the passage of time. Sikhism provides an illustration of this. Guru Nanak founded Sikhism as a religion of peace and brotherhood among all men, and the early Gurus were noted for their humility and their willingness to accept insult, and even martyrdom, with resignation. As persecution developed, the sixth Guru, Hargobind, gathered a band of warriors to fight their Mughal oppressors, and about ninety years later the tenth Guru, Gobind Singh, formed the Khalsa, a community of fearless soldier-saints. Entry into the Khalsa was to be by *Amrit*—the baptism of the sword—and the sign of membership of the Khalsa was to be the five Ks: *kesh*—uncut hair; *kangha*—comb; *kirpan*—sword; *kachs* or *kachha*—shorts; *kara*—steel bracelet, and the name Singh, meaning 'lion' (or Kaur, meaning 'princess', for a woman). The

[4] See p. 51.

46

last three Ks were directly related to the purpose for which the Khalsa had been formed—to fight for the defence of the weak and the oppressed. The shorts gave greater freedom of movement to warriors than the garment normally worn in India, and the bracelet, on the right arm, may have been worn to protect the wrist from the bowstring. Today Sikhs regard the shorts as symbolic of chastity, the sword as symbolic of their fight for truth and justice, and the steel bracelet as a symbol of strength and of the unity of Sikhs with each other and with God.

In 1972 the Sikh Missionary Society in England published a booklet by Mohinder Singh 'Cheema', called *The Sikh Bangle*. The author ascribes a wealth of symbolic meaning to the bracelet, including, in addition to the meanings mentioned above, integrity, discipline, equality, universality, eternity and humility. This is a useful illustration of the fact that we cannot pin down the meaning of an image in a neat and tidy way. Not only does it take the depth of its meaning from its context in the religion but it is capable of evoking a different response from different people as they bring to it their individual experience and their particular apprehension of the faith.

Sikhism is one of the few religions in which the adherents are likely to be able to give a reasonably precise explanation of its symbols, mainly because they are closely associated with what people do, and learning about them is an important part of a Sikh's education. In most religions, however, adherents would be hard put to it to explain in any detail the images which are a familiar part of their life. How many Christians, for instance, would be able to describe the significance of the different ways in which Christ is represented on the cross: the twisted figure hanging in agony, the robed figure with arms outstretched to the world, the crowned figure reigning from the cross, etc.?

This should not surprise us, because imagery speaks to us at a deeper level of our being than the intellectual. As in music and art and poetry our apprehension does not depend on our ability to give an academic account of it. However, it is this very quality of imagery which makes it so difficult for an outsider to gain more than a superficial understanding of its use in religion.

CONCEPT OF TIME

Another factor which makes us realize that we have entered a different world is the way in which cultures understand time, from the simple level of counting days or seasons to abstract concepts of time itself.

We are familiar with the system by which Judaism regards sunset as the beginning of a new day, a system which makes it natural to say, as the author of Genesis 1 does, 'So evening came, and morning came, the first day'. The seventh day of the week, the Sabbath, therefore begins at sunset on Friday (and ends at twilight on Saturday), and festivals begin on the 'eve' of the appropriate date. Islam also regards the evening as the beginning of a day.

Some religions observe one day in seven as a holy day but it means something different in each one. Muslims, for example, are expected to attend congregational prayers at the mosque in the early afternoon on Fridays, but it is otherwise an ordinary working day. For Jews, however, the Sabbath is separated time, a day marked off from the rest of the week. Many Christians' knowledge of Sabbath observance is confined to the command to do no work, and they sometimes transfer their own childhood memories of gloomy Sundays to the Jewish Sabbath. For Jews, however, it is a joyful day. It is a weekly celebration of the creation: 'God blessed the seventh day and made it holy, because on that day he ceased from all the work he had set himself to do' (Gen. 2.3).

The first Christians, being Jews, observed the Sabbath but in addition they met on the first day of the week to commemorate Jesus' resurrection, and eventually Sunday became their holy day instead of the Sabbath. Sunday was, of course, an ordinary working day in the Roman Empire so the Christians met for worship very early in the morning before starting the day's work.

The different ways in which Sunday is observed by Christians provide an illustration of the way in which culture and religion are intertwined. Many Protestant Christians in Britain are critical of what they call the 'continental Sunday', with its sport and other forms of entertainment. They sincerely believe that what they are trying to preserve is *the* Christian Sunday; they are unaware of the fact that it is a late development in Christian history, and that before the Puritan revolution in the seventeenth century the English Sunday was a much livelier day, with people taking part after church in such activities as dancing, ball games and watching plays being performed.

Many Hindus also observe one day in seven as a holy day, but different people keep different days, depending on which god or goddess they worship. For a Lakshmi worshipper it is Thursday; for a devotee of Kalī in Bengal, Tuesdays and Saturdays are reckoned most auspicious. Special *pūja* or prayers are offered, and many people also fast each week on the day that is consecrated to their deity.

Calendars provide another illustration of differing ways of reckoning time. There are three methods of calculating the passing of time through the year: by the sun, by the moon, or by the seasons. The third method is frequently employed by tribal peoples. An agricultural community, for example, will refer to successive seasons by names which indicate such things as the time when the ground has to be prepared, the time when seeds are sown, etc. There is no set length for these 'months'; each one is as long as is required to complete the appropriate task, but the rhythm of the seasons means that each year the cycle is completed.

Islam has a lunar calendar of twelve months, each beginning at the new moon. This means that the months gradually move round the seasons. Ramadān, the month of fasting for Muslims, will therefore fall a little earlier (about eleven days) each year, and in thirty-three years it will have rotated right through the solar year.

Judaism reckons its months by the moon as Islam does, but its years by the sun, so its months are the same length as Islam's but its years are ten or eleven days longer. Because its festivals are linked with the seasons, Tabernacles with autumn, Passover with spring, etc., it adjusts the calendar (by intercalating an extra month, called Second Adar, in seven out of every nineteen years) so that the month Tishri, for example, always falls in the September–October period, and Cheshvan in the October–November period.

Both Judaism and Islam have fixed dates for their festivals. For example, the Jewish festival of Passover begins on 15th Nisan (March–April), and the Muslim Īd al-Adhā (also transliterated Eid-al-Adhā), the great festival of sacrifice at the end of the pilgrimage to Mecca, begins on 10th Dhul-Hijja.

The dates of festivals in Hinduism and Buddhism are calculated by the moon. For example, the Theravāda Buddhist

49

festival Wesak (Vaisākha, Vesākha), which celebrates the Buddha's birth, enlightenment and death, takes place at the full moon of the month Wesak (April–May), and the Hindu festival of Divali, the festival of lights, which also marks the end of the financial year, is celebrated on the fifteenth day of the dark half of the month Kārtika (October–November).

The Christian calendar is a hybrid. The months and years are calculated by the sun. It has one major fixed festival—Christmas —but the date of Easter is calculated by the moon, and the dating of Lent which precedes it, as well as of festivals such as Ascension Day, Pentecost and Trinity Sunday, which follow it, are fixed in relation to the date of Easter.

Methods of dating years have also varied. A system of absolute dates, such as we are used to, is a relatively late invention. Earlier methods included the dating of events by the year of the reigning monarch—'in the first year of Cyrus king of Persia' (Ezra 1.1)—or by some notable happening such as an eclipse or an earthquake—'two years before the earthquake' (Amos 1.1). The Chinese reckoned years from the beginning of a dynasty, and when a new dynasty came into power they started again, counting from its first year.

The Julian calendar, as the Christian system is called, was based on calculations made by a Scythian monk in A.D. 525, but it did not come into general use until the eighth century. It took the birth of Christ as the mid-point of human history, numbering all the years 'Before Christ' backwards, and identifying all the years following as 'Anno Domini'—'In the year of our Lord'.[5]

The fact that the Julian calendar has been adopted almost universally for ease of international communication tends to obscure its specifically Christian character. We have already referred to its inappropriateness for Jews and Muslims.[6] The Muslim era is reckoned from 622 of the Christian era, but because the lunar years of the Muslim system are shorter than the solar years of the Christian system we cannot do a simple subtraction sum to find the current Muslim year. 1390 A.H. began on 9 March 1970, but the beginning of 1400 A.H. is

[5] The calendar had to be adjusted in the fifteenth century because of an error in the original calculations, so the Christian era actually dates from about four to six years after the birth of Christ.
[6] See pp. 34, 36.

50

23 November 1979. The Jewish system, which came into popular use in the ninth century C.E., begins with 3761 B.C.E. The date was calculated by rabbis on the basis of the biblical record as the beginning of the world, and the Jewish era is called the Era of Creation. The letters A.M. (Anno Mundi) are sometimes added to dates, but they are not as necessary for Jewish dating as the identifying letters are in the Christian system with its double set of dates.

Judaism, Christianity and Islam are all religions with a strong sense of the importance of history, and of the events which take place in 'time', but we turn now to two completely contrasting ways of understanding time, that of Hinduism and that of African religions.

There are two main differences between Hindu cosmology and that of Judaism, Christianity and Islam. The first is the vastness of its time scale and the second is the fact that it envisages no absolute beginning of the world and no ending. For Hindus, as for other Indian peoples, time is cyclic. They believe that the world is in a continuous state of dissolution and recreation. What Westerners find it almost impossible to imagine is the length of the cycles. The shortest cycle is called a *mahāyuga* (great age or aeon). It is made up of four *yugas*. The first, which is the most perfect age, lasts for 1,728,000 years. There is a gradual deterioration through the four ages. Righteousness declines and men live shorter and less happy lives. The fourth age, the *kali-yuga*, is the shortest—432,000 years—and things are at their worst. Hindus believe that we are living in a *kali-yuga*, which is popularly thought to have begun in 3102 B.C. At the end of a *kali-yuga* the world is destroyed by fire and water. A *mahāyuga*, however, is only a short cycle. One thousand *mahāyugas* make up one *kalpa*. A *kalpa* is known as a 'day of Brahmā'.[7] It lasts for 4,320,000,000 years, and it is followed by a 'night of Brahmā', which lasts for a similar period. At the end of a day of Brahmā the universe is dissolved and is not re-created till the end of the night of Brahmā. Three hundred and sixty of these days and nights of Brahmā make up a year of Brahmā, who lives for a hundred years. At the end of this time Brahmā himself is dissolved along with the universe, and there is a period of

---

[7] Brahmā is the personified creator God.

51

quiescence until the emergence of a new Brahmā, and the whole cyclic process begins again.[8]

It is against this background that we have to understand the concept of *samsāra*, the endless round of rebirths which is the fate of all living beings who have not achieved enlightenment. Because our Western minds cannot take in the numbers involved in the ever-recurring cycles we are tempted to imagine that a person might have to be reborn tens of times, or perhaps even hundreds of times, before achieving *moksha*, release. The expression 'countless rebirths' is virtually impossible for us to grasp.

The Indian religions claim, with some justification that modern science's revelations about the age of the universe have not been a problem for them, in contrast to the disruptive effect they have had on Western religions with their relatively short time scale.

We turn now to a completely different way of looking at time. For the African time is not cyclic, but neither is it linear in the sense of stretching back to a beginning and forward to an ending. History moves backward from the present, and it has virtually no future. In *African Religions and Philosophy* John Mbiti states that in his research into East African languages he found no words or expressions which convey the idea of a distant future, and he illustrates the distinctive African concept of time by an analysis of the verb tenses used in two of the languages.[9] For each of the nine tenses he gives the approximate time they refer to:

1 Far future: about two to six months from now.
2 Immediate future: within the next short while.
3 Indefinite future: within a forseeable while, after such and such an event.
4 Present: now.
5 Immediate past: in the last hour or so.
6 Today's past: from the time of rising up to about two hours ago.
7 Recent past: yesterday.

[8] The length of these periods of time has symbolical rather than literal significance, and considerable variation can be found in the number of years ascribed to each.
[9] p. 18.

8 Far past: any day before yesterday.
9 Unspecified past: no specific time in the past.

Africans have no interest in calculating time. Events are more important than numbers and dates, but for events to be regarded as significant they must be experienced or be near enough in the future to be within reach of being experienced. Once events have happened they live in the memory of those who have experienced them, whether of individuals or of communities. They are then, however, always receding, moving backwards in time, and once there is no one left who remembers them they disappear into unspecified time—*Zamani*. John Mbiti says: 'Zamani becomes a period beyond which nothing can go. Zamani is ... the final storehouse for all phenomena and events, the ocean of time in which everything becomes absorbed into a reality that is neither after nor before ... Zamani is the period of the myth.'[10]

Myth is profoundly significant in African religions. If we fail to grasp this relationship between event, experience and myth we could easily make the grave error of regarding African myths as little more than interesting tales.

The African concept of time is as different from our Western way of thinking as is the Hindu one, and yet the African and Hindu concepts are startlingly different from each other. At first sight words like beginning, ending, past, present, future, appear to be much more straightforward than words like *avatāra*, *torah* and *dharma*, but they turn out to be just as much a part of our cultural heritage as 'incarnation' and 'law' and 'teaching'. To understand another religion is indeed to enter a different world.

[10] Op. cit., p. 23.

6

IN CONTEXT

When we choose a cross-cultural approach to the study of religions rather than concentrating on one religion, we have to be particularly on our guard against the danger of distortion which results from looking at aspects of religions out of their proper context.

One illustration of this is provided by the craze for Yoga which has swept through the West in recent years. Encouraged by television programmes and articles in the press, most people think that Yoga is nothing more than a set of exercises designed to make one healthier and more relaxed. Some Yoga teachers do in fact tell their classes that the physical exercises are only part of a much larger system of spiritual discipline, but unless people already know something of the Indian religious tradition from which Yoga comes they tend not to 'hear' the explanation, and so Yoga becomes just the latest in a long line of 'keep fit' activities.

Perhaps this does not matter. If these particular exercises are beneficial that is all right. What is wrong is the assumption that they constitute the Indian practice of Yoga.

The word *yoga* comes from a root meaning 'yoke', with both connotations of the English word—'unite' or 'join', and 'harness' or 'discipline'. It can be used in a number of ways, but all have a profound religious meaning. One of them is found in the Bhagavad-Gītā, which describes three paths to salvation: *karma-yoga*, the way or discipline of work, doing one's duty, *jñānayoga*, the way of wisdom or knowledge, and *bhaktiyoga*, the way of devotion to Krishna. The use of the word that we are more familiar with is as the name of a set of religious practices which include moral elements and meditation as well as the physical elements which have been imported into the West. It is one of the methods employed by Hindus, Buddhists and Jains to develop the control of the passions and the mental and physical discipline which are essential stages on man's journey towards liberation.

In the days before anthropology developed into the scientific study we know today, anthropologists were dependent for their data on travellers' tales, accounts supplied by missionaries, and any other descriptions which came their way. They are known as 'armchair anthropologists', because they did not undertake field studies themselves and they were seldom able to check their sources even if they had felt it to be necessary. This method of collecting data produced a vast but haphazard assortment of anecdotal material. It was often of a spectacular kind because those who supplied it thought that a community's everyday activities were not worth reporting. It therefore existed in a vacuum, completely unrelated to its context. An anthropologist would sort through his 'rag-bag' of accounts of customs to find suitable material for the theories he was working on. In many of the studies published in the latter part of the nineteenth century and the first two decades of this one apparently similar customs and practices of peoples from widely differing parts of the world were grouped together, with the assumption that the peoples must have held the same beliefs.

External similarities, however, may conceal quite different inner meaning. Cremation, for example, is practised by Hindus and it is also practised by some Christians, but its significance is different in the two religions. In Hinduism the practice goes back to the early Vedic period (c. 1500–1000 B.C.), where it was associated with Agni, the God of Fire, who consumed the physical body after death, taking the soul to heaven. Hinduism has undergone many changes since the Vedic period, including the introduction of the belief in reincarnation, but fire, still regarded as sacred, plays a central part in religious rituals. Cremation is a comparatively recent practice for Christians. Disposal of the dead has traditionally been by burial in the earth—'Dust you are, to dust you shall return' (Gen. 3.19). Cremation was introduced for reasons of hygiene and scarcity of land; it does not reflect basic religious beliefs in the way that cremation does for Hindus and burial does for Christians.

Although the 'rag-bag' approach has long been discredited in the world of scholarship it has shown signs of reappearing in some of the books written for use in religious education, under the mistaken impression that it is phenomenological. The expression 'phenomenology of religion' is used in several different ways, but one of them refers to a method whereby the phenomena, or empirical data, of religions are studied and a comparison is made of the same phenomena, e.g. initiation rites or prayer, in different religions. We may note two important characteristics of this method. The first is that no judgement is made about the truth or falsity of beliefs (the Greek word *epochē* is used for this suspension of judgement). The second is that the aim of the study is to get at the meaning of the beliefs and practices for the adherents of the religion, and this can be accomplished only by seeing them in their context in the religion as a whole.

We have to treat with great caution, therefore, any books which merely describe customs drawn at random from tribal communities and world religions, and which make little or no attempt to help us to see the meaning of the customs for those who practise them.

If we want to study the phenomenon of pilgrimages it is not enough merely to discover that Muslims make a pilgrimage to the holy city of Mecca at least once in their lifetime, in fulfilment of one of the five Pillars of Islam, that Hindus go on pilgrimage to places associated with some deity, a temple or other shrine, and particularly to the sacred city of Benares, and so on. For a real understanding of pilgrimages we need the answer to such questions as: Does the journey itself have any significance, or only the goal at the end of the journey? What kind of worship, if any, is offered? What is the pilgrim's attitude of mind as he approaches the object of his worship? What is the nature of the blessings he expects to receive from his pilgrimage? How does he regard the sacrifices he has to make or the hardships he has to undergo? What is the significance for him of the rituals he performs, the words he uses, the garments he wears? Why in some religions, e.g. in Islam, is the pilgrimage confined to adherents of the religion, while in others, e.g. in Hinduism, anyone may take part?[1] Why would it be misleading to put Lourdes

[1] There is a vivid and moving account by a Christian monk of his experience on a pilgrimage to the source of the sacred river Ganges in 'The Mountain of the Lord', one of two stories in *Guru and Disciple* by Abhishiktānanda (S.P.C.K. 1974). See also Klaus Klostermaier, *Hindu and Christian in Vrindaban* (S.C.M. Press 1969), for an account of another Christian priest's sojourn at a Hindu pilgrimage centre associated with Krishna.

56

and Mecca in the same category of places to which pilgrimage is made?

Beliefs as well as customs belong among the phenomena of religion, and the most difficult beliefs for outsiders to comprehend are a religion's concepts of God. What do we make, for instance, of the Hindu concept of deity? Our ideas of what are the appropriate attributes and activities for a deity have been so shaped by our own cultural background that we find it difficult either to understand or to appreciate beliefs about deities which differ radically from our own.

In addition, the language used to describe deities has a significance within a religion which is not obvious to outsiders. Muslims, for example, find it impossible to believe the Christian claim to monotheism. After all, Christians not only use the expression 'three persons' about God, but their creeds affirm quite explicitly 'I believe in one God the Father Almighty ... And in one Lord Jesus Christ ... And I believe in the Holy Ghost', and they address prayers to Jesus and to the Holy Spirit as well as to God the Father. How many Christians, though, could explain how these examples really do reflect a belief in only one God? A salutary reminder that difficulties of understanding exist for adherents of religions as well as for those outside.

It might have been expected that the Christian experience of a monotheistic belief expressed in ways which suggest tritheism to non-Christians would have made it easier for Christians to understand Hinduism. In fact, Christians seem to have had more difficulty in comprehending Hinduism's concepts of deity than those of many other religions. One of the problems is the range of beliefs to be found within Hinduism; another is its fluidity, so that it is impossible to draw hard and fast lines between the different sets of beliefs which have all found a home within the hospitable compass of the religion; and yet another is its concept of the unity of all being, with a resulting blurring of the distinctions—so marked in Christian theology—between gods and men and the rest of the animal kingdom.

At one time it was popularly believed in the West that Hinduism was polytheistic, with a pantheon of gods and goddesses so large that it couldn't even be counted. More recently, particularly since the writings of intellectual Hindus have become known in Europe and North America, it has been believed by many that Hinduism is monistic, with the Absolute conceived

57

of as an impersonal divine reality underlying the universe, and the 'soul' of man being identical with the Absolute. It has therefore been confusing for many to discover that not only do both these beliefs exist but that monotheism is one of the strongest strands in Hinduism.

Bald statements about Vaishnavites worshipping Vishnu and Shaivites worshipping Shiva do not go far towards explaining the monotheism, especially when it is realized that Vaishnavites may also worship Shiva and Brahmā, and Shaivites may also worship Vishnu and Brahmā. When we are told that Vishnu is the personal name of the supreme Being for Vaishnavites, as Shiva is for Shaivites, and that other deities are regarded as attributes of the supreme Being, we have taken one step towards understanding, but considerable study both of historical developments within Hinduism and of the different groups in India today lies ahead of us before we can say with any confidence that we have grasped something of Hindu concepts of deity.

PARTS AND WHOLES

In Chapter 3 we considered the fact that all religions (except primal ones) exist in a variety of forms, and this raises another problem. When is it safe to draw general conclusions about a religion from the part of it which we are studying? Two English teenagers were being interviewed recently in a radio programme on Buddhism, but neither they nor their interviewer seemed to be aware that what they were talking about with such enthusiasm was Zen Buddhism—and a very anglicized form of Zen at that—and that practically nothing of what they said applied to Theravāda Buddhism or even to the other Mahāyāna schools.

We are likely to meet the problem in its most acute form when our study of a religion is part of a wider study of a particular country or region. For example, Iran is a Muslim country but most Iranian Muslims are Shī'as, while orthodox Islam is Sunni (see page 21), so it would be wrong to generalize from some of the aspects of the religion we found there. We could marvel at the beauty of Persian art, including scenes with Muhammad (suitably haloed) and his followers, and not know that in mainstream Islam it has been forbidden to represent sentient beings, i.e. animals or humans, and particularly the

Prophet Muhammad, because of the danger of idolatry.

Similarly, in a study of Eire we might come to the conclusion that the Roman Catholic Church is a conservative force, but if our study were of one of the Latin American countries where priests have aligned themselves with the socialists working for the liberation of the poor and the oppressed—apparently so effectively that some priests and seminary students have been murdered by right-wing terrorist groups—we might come to the conclusion that the Roman Catholic Church is a revolutionary movement. We would also discover that in Latin America many Christians who are extreme left wing politically are evangelicals, though our experience of the Christian Church in our own country would probably save us from jumping too hastily to conclusions about the political allegiance of all evangelicals.

When we use literature produced by the adherents of a religion it is important to ask which group it has emanated from. Is it Orthodox or Reform Judaism? Is it Theravāda or Zen or Pure Land or Tibetan Buddhism? Does it come from one of the mainstream groups, like those just mentioned, or from a minor sect? Although the major groups are likely to be reasonably tolerant of each other, in most religions there are sects which are regarded as heretical by the main groups. This applies especially in Islam and Christianity, which have been particularly concerned with orthodoxy. All sects, however small or however extreme their variations from the parent religion, consider themselves to be the true representatives of the faith. Their literature often claims to speak for the religion as a whole, and we certainly should not expect to find them using the word 'heretical' about themselves!

Another area in which it is all too easy to mistake the part for the whole is sacred writings. It can happen when we don't know the original context of a passage, that is, the situation for which, or out of which, it was written, and it can happen when we don't know the relationship of a passage to its wider context in the writings or in the religion as a whole.

One illustration of this is the disapproving attitude which Christians have persistently shown towards the injunction about polygamy in the Qur'ān (Sūra 4.3). It has been seen as according a low status to women in Islam. It is not easy to reconstruct in detail the social conditions in Arabia in Muhammad's time, but some things are clear. First, the injunction follows a verse about

59

making certain that orphans are not defrauded of their property. Verse 3 begins, 'If you fear that you will not act justly towards the orphans, marry such women as seem good to you, two, three, four'. The sūra dates from the Medina period, when many women and girls had been widowed or orphaned by the death in battle of numbers of Muhammad's followers. Muhammad was concerned that provision should be made for those who would otherwise be unprotected in society. Secondly, the injunction continues, 'but if you fear you will not be equitable, then only one ...' Some Muslims in later centuries, sensitive to the Christian charge about polygamy, have suggested that because the ability to treat two or more wives absolutely fairly is beyond the powers of human nature, the injunction is really a command to monogamy. Most Muslims, however, reject this interpretation.

If we see this injunction in the wider context of the Qur'ān, we find that Muhammad's legislation gave to women a greatly improved position in society. For example, the marriage dowry had to be paid to the bride herself and not to her father, the consent of a woman was required for a marriage contract, and the rights of women in the inheritance of property were guaranteed. The Islamic legislation marked a definite raising of the status of women in seventh-century Arabia.

Another illustration of the problem of context is the polemical passages about other religions which can be found in some scriptures and which give a misleading impression of the views held by the religion today. Judaism, for example, is one of the most tolerant religions in its attitude to other faiths. It does not seek to make converts; it does not ask other men to take on themselves the 'yoke of the Law' or the suffering which mankind continually inflicts on the Jewish community. It believes that the Noachite laws[2] were given by God to humanity and that salvation is open to all who live moral lives. Yet in its Bible there are many fierce attacks on the religion of the Canaanites, the Phoenicians, the Assyrians, the Babylonians, etc.

It would be quite wrong to 'read off' Judaism's attitude to other religions from these passages. We see them in perspective when we realize that they belong to the far distant past, and to a

---

[2] The rabbis taught that seven commands had been given to the sons of Noah, i.e. to all mankind: to practise justice, and to refrain from blasphemy, murder, robbery, idolatry, sexual perversion, and eating the flesh of a living creature. (Sanh. 56a.)

time when the existence of Israel and the people's fidelity to their God were threatened by assimilation to the ways of other nations. The efforts of the prophets and other leaders to prevent the apostasy of their own people, however, led them to pour scorn on the gods of other nations and to represent their worship in negative terms.

We should hardly expect the Jewish scriptures to produce the most accurate account of the religions which were attacked in this way. Surprisingly though, biblical scholars used the Bible as their main source of information about these religions until increasing knowledge of the ancient Near East, and particularly the discoveries of archaeology, caused many of their ideas to be revised. It was long believed, for example, that the Canaanites had a very primitive type of religion and that they worshipped nameless local deities—baals—at their village shrines. The discoveries at Ugarit (modern Ras Shamra) in 1929 revealed that the religion of the Canaanites, even before the entry of the Israelites into Canaan after the Exodus from Egypt, was much more sophisticated than the references to it in the Bible would suggest. It had an extensive literature, and a pantheon of deities (of whom one was called Baal) with distinctive attributes and well-defined relationships with each other.

The polemical passages about Judaism in the New Testament also have to be seen in their context. They reflect the conflict which arose between official Judaism and the followers of 'The Way', later called Christians, who claimed that they alone were the true Israel. As we saw in Chapter 4, we would not expect to use the New Testament as our main source of information about Judaism.

A passage can give a misleading impression of carrying scriptural authority when it is taken out of its proper context. We are familiar with the practice of using proof-texts, by which people sometimes seek to justify their particular beliefs. They quote isolated verses, frequently irrespective of which part of the scriptures they come from, as 'proof' of scriptural support for their beliefs, whether these are about the dangers of alcohol or the imminent end of the world, the wrath of God or the existence of a personal devil. Their opponents, of course, can equally easily find other verses to support contrary beliefs. In our study of the scriptures of religions we must be careful not to base our ideas about what people believe on the evidence

61

of isolated passages. We have to check the content of such passages against the overall beliefs of the religion.

Our task is made more complicated by the fact that the principle of selectivity is not confined to the popular level of quoting proof-texts; the major groups within a religion may well interpret their scriptures in different ways. This results not from ignorance of what is in the literature, but rather from a difference in judgement about where it is right to put the emphasis. All scriptures are interpreted writings, and every religion has its army of scholars who wrestle with the meaning of the writings, and who write commentaries for their fellow believers. The different sections of the Christian Church frequently claim scriptural authority for the things which divide them, and the rise of new movements within Christianity is always accompanied by a claim to be returning to a scriptural basis, whether this refers to the nature of baptism, the role of church officers, prophecies about the millennium, or the kind of behaviour expected of church members.

The classical example of interpreted sacred writings comes from Hinduism. Scholars of varying traditions have studied the Bhagavad-Gītā and written commentaries on it. Two of the most interesting are Shankara, in the ninth century A.D., and Rāmānuja, two centuries later. Shankara was the great exponent of monism. He taught the essential unity of Ātman, the self, with Brahman, ultimate Reality, and salvation as man's realization that his eternal self or soul is none other than Brahman. Shankara allowed that devotion to a personal God might be necessary for many people, but said that the aim was to pass beyond the stage of piety and devotion, for they belonged to the illusion that the world consisted of separate entities. Shankara claimed that the Bhagavad-Gītā was consistent with the beliefs he expounded. But so did Rāmānuja, the scholar who was so influential in the development of the *bhakti* (devotional) movement in Hinduism. Rāmānuja claimed that the way of knowledge which Shankara saw as the true path to salvation was inadequate. He taught that the Absolute was personal, and that, although man was of the same essence as God, his destiny was a union with God in which the soul yet retained its identity. (Rāmānuja's system is for this reason called Qualified Non-dualism.) Man's devotion to God, which was in response to

God's grace offered to man, was the highest possible state of bliss.

What are we to make of the Bhagavad-Gītā when two of the greatest Hindu scholars have written commentaries on it and yet interpret it so differently? We should not be too disturbed by this. We are studying actual religions, not simplistic accounts of religions, and our study should always include something of the main ways in which sacred writings have been interpreted within the religions themselves.

WHOSE?

One of the most fascinating questions about context arises when we find something which is shared by more than one religion.

It can happen with places. Jerusalem, for instance, has particular religious significance for Judaism, for Christianity and for Islam, though the significance is far from identical. The original significance of a place often gets overlaid as it develops other associations during its history. This certainly applies to the tensions between Jews and Muslims over Jerusalem. As we have already seen, religions do not exist in a vacuum, and it is impossible to disentangle them from the political history of the nation in which they are to be found. This was illustrated vividly at a conference in England of Jews, Muslims and Christians. The members were not specialists in dialogue, but ordinary men and women who had come together to try to increase their understanding of each other's faiths. Everyone was taking great care to say nothing which would be offensive to another community and the conference seemed to be going well. It was a surprise therefore to hear one of the Muslim members expressing extreme frustration about the fact that in his discussion group the Jewish members were continually referring to Israel. He was unfamiliar with the use of the word for the people of Israel down the ages; to him it meant only one thing—the modern state of Israel.

Sometimes festivals are shared by two religions. Sikhism, originating in India, still observes the festivals of Holī and Divali, but we would be wrong to assume that they have the same meaning for the Sikhs that they have for the Hindus. With their rejection of the gods of Hinduism Sikhs certainly would not want to identify themselves with the worship of Krishna and

Lakshmī associated with the festivals. Rather, they regard Holī and Divali as holiday occasions, with the emphasis on the cultural and recreational aspects. They have, however, given Divali a distinctive Sikh significance: they celebrate the release from prison of the sixth Guru, Hargobind, which took place at the time of a Divali festival. Holī and Divali, which are two of the most important festivals in Hinduism, are not nearly as important in the Sikh calendar as Baisakhi, which commemorates the founding of the Khalsa by Guru Gobind Singh, or even the birthdays of Guru Nanak and Guru Gobind Singh and the martyrdoms of Guru Arjan Dev and Guru Teg Bahadur.

Sometimes two religions share part of their history and part of their scriptures, and then the question of setting events, beliefs and practices in their right context becomes crucial. The classic example of this shared heritage is Judaism and Christianity. The first Christians were Jews who believed that God's promises to his people had been fulfilled in their generation in the person of Jesus of Nazareth, and they saw no reason to discard the scriptures which enshrined those promises. As Christopher Evans puts it: 'Christianity is unique among the great religions in being born with a Bible in its cradle'.[3] The Christians naturally put more emphasis on those parts of the scriptures which supported their beliefs, and as they gradually broke away from Judaism and formed a separate religion so they differed more and more in their interpretation of biblical passages. The beginnings of this process can be seen in the writings of the New Testament, where passages in the Old Testament are seen through Christian 'spectacles'. (Cf. the application of the words of the prophet Joel to the Christian experience of the outpouring of the Spirit at Pentecost, and the application of Psalm 22 and Isaiah 53 to Jesus.)

Christians don't seem to have been able to come to terms with the fact that Judaism still has its Bible, interpreted within its own community of faith. This was illustrated during a course of lectures on world religions. The audience listened with respectful interest to the accounts of Islam and Buddhism. Then it was the turn of Judaism. The lecturer said that he wanted to begin with one of the most important concepts in Judaism—the Covenant. When he finished the audience attacked him vigorously. Everyone who spoke, including two ordained Christians,

[3] *Is 'Holy Scripture' Christian?* (S.C.M. Press 1971), p. 2.

64

explained to him that he had got it wrong; that was not what Covenant meant!

It is this divergence of interpretation which makes nonsense of a practice which used to be followed in some schools in predominantly Jewish areas. Teachers would explain cheerfully that they solved the religious education problem by doing 'only the Old Testament'.

The attitude of Muslims to the Jewish and Christian scriptures is similar to the attitude of Christians to the Jewish Bible. The Jewish and Christian scriptures do not of course comprise part of the Qur'ān in the way that the Jewish Bible comprises a (very large) part of the Christian Bible, but they do have some material in common. There are many references, for example, to characters like Abraham and Moses. Muslims believe that their religion is not a new one, but that the same revelation of God was given to a succession of prophets or messengers, the first of whom was the first man, Adam. They believe that this revelation was given as the Torah to Moses for the Jews, and as the Gospel to Jesus for the Christians, but that their followers altered or concealed parts of it. Finally, to ensure that the message would not be corrupted, God revealed it to Muhammad in the form of the Qur'ān.

The Muslim explanation of the fate of the earlier revelations would account for variations in the common material. References to Abraham, for instance, include the account of his willingness to sacrifice Ishmael, not Isaac (Sūra 37.103.)[4]

Abraham has an honoured place in Islam. He is called *muslim* because he surrendered to the will of God. He is also called 'the *Hanīf*', or Monotheist, because of his worship of Allāh and his rejection of the gods of his father. Sūra 21.52ff. tells how he broke all but the largest of the idols which his father and his kinsfolk worshipped. When he was questioned about it he said that the chief idol had done it, and he told the people to ask the other idols. When they replied that idols cannot speak Abraham demanded to know why, then, they worshipped idols instead of Allāh. This story does not appear in the Judaeo-Christian scriptures, but there is a Jewish midrash[5] which tells how Abraham broke his father's gods with a hatchet and then

[4] Traditionally the ancestry of the Jews has been traced back to Abraham through Isaac and that of the Arabs through Ishmael.

[5] Commentary on the biblical material.

65

put the hatchet into the hands of the biggest of them. When his father Terah asked Abraham what he had done to his gods Abraham said that the biggest one took the hatchet and broke them all.

In Islam Jesus is regarded as the last and greatest of the prophets apart from Muhammad himself. Muslims' attitude to him is one of reverence and they frequently say 'Peace be upon him' when they speak about him as they do at the mention of Muhammad's name. In the Qur'ān he is usually referred to as 'Jesus son of Mary'. Muslims deny completely that he was the Son of God. They are fierce monotheists, and to associate any-one with God is the greatest sin. They do, however, accept the virgin birth. The Qur'ān includes accounts of the annunciation and the birth of Jesus, and references to his disciples, his miracles, etc. Muslims believe that Jesus was not crucified; it only appeared that he had been, but God had taken him to himself (Sūra 4.156). They also claim that when Jesus promised that the Comforter would come after him he was referring to Muhammad.

It will be obvious from the illustrations we have looked at that where anything is shared by two religions we cannot make a simple transfer of meaning from one to the other. Similar illustrations could be drawn from the Indian religious traditions and from the religions of Japan, but for Christians at least the place of Jesus in Islam is probably the most vivid reminder that if we want to understand what something means to the adherents of a religion we have to study it in the context of that religion.

7

PROGRESS OR DECLINE?

It is one of the facts of the universe that to be alive means to be subject to change. Anything which has ceased to respond to its environment is dead. It should not surprise us, therefore, that religions change and develop. If they were nothing more than an intellectual game or a haven for neurotics they might be able to exist in relative isolation from what is happening in the rest of the world, but they are concerned with the whole of man's life.[1]

It is not without significance that expressions which indicate this concern with how men live are common among religions. Judaism's Law is called *Halakhah*, which means 'to walk', and the Hebrew word for road, *derek*, is the word which is found in the expression 'the way of the Lord'. The first Christians were known as followers of 'The Way'. The Muslim system of law is called the *Sharī'a*, which means 'road' or 'highway'. Hindus speak of different 'paths' (*mārga*) to liberation. Buddhism is called the Middle Way, and Buddhists have for their guidance the Supreme Eight-fold Path. Taoism takes its name from *Tao*, which means 'way' or 'road'. Religious beliefs have to be reflected in what a man does. Man lives in the world, and the religious community to which he belongs exists in the world, subject to all its economic, social, political and international pressures.

Religions may respond to changing situations in quite different ways, and it is not possible to predict in advance what the response will be. To take an extreme example, some religions, or sections of religions, have virtually been wiped out by persecution; in other cases the blood of the martyrs really has been the seed of the Church (to borrow a popular Christian expression), and the religions have emerged even stronger from the fires of persecution.

[1] One of the most important contemporary causes of development, inter-religious dialogue (using 'dialogue' in its broadest sense), will be referred to in Chapters 9 and 10.

In our study we have to be aware of, and try to understand, developments in religions. In this chapter we shall look at four of the ways in which they develop: through evolution, through reformation, through schism and through the creation of new religions. These are obviously overlapping categories. They are useful in that they indicate different emphases, but they must not be thought of as making hard and fast distinctions.

EVOLUTION

To evolve means to develop new forms from existing ones. It suggests gradual change, but not necessarily improvement. In the late nineteenth century the word 'evolution' acquired ethical overtones. Darwin's discoveries had shown that life had evolved from simple forms into more complex ones. Man, at the end of the process, naturally assumed that he was superior to all other forms of life. The description of one of the ways by which species evolved—the survival of the fittest—was also taken over from biology and applied in other spheres, such as economics, the social structure, and race relations in the empire's colonial possessions. It was assumed that those who survived most successfully must have been the fittest (morally speaking) to do so.

The study of religions was no exception to the practice of equating evolution with progress. The simpler the form of a religion was (or at least appeared to be), the lower down the scale it was placed, and many Christian scholars attempted to show how Christianity was the climax and end product of the long process of evolution, from primitive fear and superstition to a religion of faith and love.[2]

During the twentieth century we have had to jettison such simplistic judgements. For example, more accurate knowledge has resulted in a complete reappraisal of 'primitive' religions. Not only are they much more complex than was previously imagined, but they include some aspects, such as a strong sense of community, which 'civilized' man might well envy. Evolution

[2] It is interesting to reflect that their placing of Christianity at the end of the process does not seem to have been disturbed by the fact that other religions developed after Christianity, particularly Islam, with its overt claim to be the climax and final form of religion for mankind.

is not necessarily progress, as the dinosaurs discovered to their cost. Some developments are good, some are not, and opinion will always be divided about the appropriateness of specific developments, in religion as in everything else.

Institutions are one aspect of religion in which evolution takes place. Once a religion expands beyond a small, close-knit community it requires machinery for communication between the scattered parts, for the training and authorization of its recognized priests or teachers, and for the administration of funds and other resources. Eastern religions have managed to keep their institutional life to a minimum, but the religions which put a greater emphasis on centralization have found that institutions develop in a dinosaur-like way. Christianity, for example, has assemblies and synods, conferences and councils, educational institutions, charitable organizations, and publications, not to mention committees for relations with secular institutions, with other denominations within the faith, and with religions outside it.

Some people are provoked to protest that the 'simple faith' has been lost sight of under the structures. Others point to the fact that the Gospel is concerned with the wholeness of man's life and that without structures it would not be possible, for example, for Christian Aid to collect and distribute funds for the relief of human need, nor would it be possible for members of the Church to make any contribution to the decision-making process. From time to time there are experiments with new forms of church life at the local level, for example, house groups or communes. Whether the new forms will supplement the more conventional structures or whether they will eventually replace them, only time can tell.

Forms of worship evolve much more slowly than institutions. This is to be expected. Worship is the approach of man to the deity, and it has always taken carefully prescribed forms. The forms have varied widely, but each religion or sect has had no doubts about the rightness of its particular form. Throughout history it has been believed that the well-being of man and, in some religions, even the order and harmony of the universe, have depended on the correct performance of sacrifices and other rituals. The control of worship and the knowledge of the rituals have traditionally been in the hands of the priestly class—a group not normally thought of as enthusiastic innovators. Moreover, for ordinary worshippers the familiar rituals have provided not only a sense of stability in the present, but a sense of continuity with the past.

While only minor modifications in worship are likely to be recommended, even in these days, by the officials of a religion (in spite of some vociferous protests, changes in Christian worship such as those in the Roman Catholic Mass or the Church of England's Series 3 services can hardly be described as revolutionary), it is religious leaders who are mainly responsible for the evolution of doctrines. Christians can see this process at work in the New Testament itself, as writers like Paul and John and the author of the Epistle to the Hebrews wrestle with the implications of the newly developed faith, and in the fourth century A.D. it was theologians like Athanasius and Arius who battled over the doctrine of the person of Christ.

Even in the field of doctrine, however, evolution is likely to take place only slowly. In any community conservative forces tend to be more numerous than radical ones, and there will always be people who resist any alteration to the *status quo* on principle, as well as those who oppose a particular change on the basis of an informed judgement about it.

Judaism is one of the few religions to have consciously attempted to combine both the traditions of the past and adaptation to new situations. This balancing feat is not without its problems, and some groups, such as the Reform movement, have leaned more towards adaptation to the present situation, while the Hassidic and ultra-Orthodox groups have leaned more towards the maintenance of traditions.

Adaptation is no new process in Judaism. Nearly two and a half thousand years ago the need to apply the Mosaic Law in situations very different from those for which it was originally promulgated was met by the development of the oral Law. A class of learned men arose, whose task it was to study and interpret the written Law and give guidance on its contemporary application. This process still continues today. (See page 88.)

Sometimes developments occur in response to changed political situations. We have already noted the development of Sikhism into a brotherhood of warriors under pressure from the Mughal rulers of India in the seventeenth century. (See page 46.) Some developments are small and precise, like the alteration made by Muhammad in the direction to which Muslims turned for prayer.

At first they faced Jerusalem, but the original close relationship with the Jewish community at Medina deteriorated, and it was at this time that Muhammad received the inspiration that Muslims should face Mecca.

A changed political situation may, however, have far-reaching consequences, like those which followed the conversion to Christianity of the Emperor Constantine at the beginning of the fourth century. From being a persecuted minority the Christian Church became the established religion of the Roman Empire—and acquired in the process all the trappings of a worldly power. The conversion of the Emperor Ashoka to Buddhism in the third century B.C.E. was likewise a turning point in that religion's history. Under the emperor's patronage Buddhism not only flourished, but it began the missionary expansion which took it beyond India to Sri Lanka in the south, and eventually to China, Japan and South-East Asia.

Sometimes a religious community is deeply divided about what its response should be in a particular situation. This happened to the Christian community in Japan during the Second World War. As the country came under increasing pressure from its enemies, and the need for national unity became of paramount importance, the government declared that the Christian Churches would be allowed to remain in existence if they joined in the ceremonies at the shrines of the official religion, State Shinto. What should they do? Some Christians argued that the ceremony at the shrine was a mere formality which did not affect their faith; it was better to make the gesture than sacrifice the work the Churches were doing. Others maintained that any participation, however perfunctory, in Shinto ceremonies would be interpreted as sharing Shinto beliefs, and their own witness would be compromised, so they refused to comply with the government's order, and took the consequences.

Some of the most striking developments in religions occur when they are transplanted into other countries. Christianity originated in the Semitic culture of the Middle East, but within a century or two it had become established in the countries around the Mediterranean—Asia Minor, Greece, Italy, North Africa—and it developed distinctive customs and ways of thinking in each of them.

Even national temperament can make religions develop in different directions. The phlegmatic approach of Christians in

71

northern Europe differs from the more volatile approach of their counterparts in countries like Spain and Italy, while the exuberance of the peoples of the West Indies finds expression as naturally in their Christian worship and festivals as in activities like cricket and carnivals. West Indian immigrants to Britain have suffered a profound shock to find in Christian worship what seems to them to be extreme coldness and lack of feeling.

Religions may undergo more fundamental transformations when they take root in other countries. Zen, one of the schools of Japanese Buddhism, is an obvious example. It originated in the twelfth century when the teachings of Ch'an Buddhism were introduced into Japan,[3] but it soon developed a distinctive Japanese character. This can be seen in such things as the elaborate ritual of the tea ceremony and the austere and serene beauty of the gardens created from natural forms—rocks, trees and streams. Perhaps the most surprising aspect of Zen Buddhism was its use of the martial arts—sword play and archery—as part of its discipline, and its popularity among the *samurai*, that stern warrior class who flourished in the mediaeval period.

The introduction of Eastern religions into Europe and America in recent years has also demonstrated the way in which adaptations take place. The saffron-robed members of the Krishna Consciousness movement, jogging along the street chanting 'Hare Krishna', have become a familiar sight in many Western cities. Many of the young converts, however, conscious of the reality of the experience which has transformed their lives, believe that Krishna Consciousness is *the* truth for all men, and in their missionary zeal some of them resort to the kind of high pressure evangelism which has more in common with certain sections of the Christian Church than with the Hinduism they have espoused.

At a more fundamental level, doctrine has developed in new and distinctive ways when it has emerged from the life of a religion in a different cultural setting. The obvious example here is Mahāyāna Buddhism, which has produced a succession of Buddhist scholars in the lands to which it has spread. They have not all been concerned with the same areas of scholarship.

---

[3] Zen is the Japanese pronunciation of the Chinese word 'Ch'an', which in turn is the Chinese pronunciation of the Sanskrit word *dhyāna*, meaning 'meditation'.

For example, Buddhist schools of philosophy developed in India, alongside and frequently in debate with the Hindu schools of philosophy. In China, however, philosophy never became a major concern of Buddhist scholars, whose great contribution, to the religion as a whole and not only to Chinese Buddhism, was the translation and intensive study of Buddhist texts.

REFORMATION

As we noted at the beginning of the chapter, evolution does not exclude reform, but we are using the word 'reformation' to refer to intentional developments which bring about a significant change in direction in a religion.

Reformation may be accomplished by religious leaders. This happened in Judaism in the fifth to fourth centuries B.C.E., when Ezra established the community in Judah on the basis of the written Law and a rigid policy of separatism. As with all reformations it is possible to trace developments in earlier periods, and the exile of the Jews in Babylon in the sixth century B.C.E. created a situation in which law became important in the everyday life of the people as the community attempted both to maintain its faithfulness to the God of Israel in a strange land and to retain its identity for half a century in the face of threatened assimilation. However, the decisive steps which caused these developments to become firmly rooted in the religion were taken by Ezra, with the help of his contemporary, Nehemiah. The reformation they accomplished was so effective that an ordered and disciplined way of life has been a feature of Judaism ever since, and the importance of the Law for everyday living created a tradition of the study and interpretation of the Law that lies at the very heart of the religion. (See pages 87f.)

The twentieth century has witnessed a remarkable reformation within Christianity, initiated by the leadership of the Roman Catholic Church. Pope John XXIII summoned the Second Vatican Council, which met in Rome for two months a year from 1962 to 1965. Its influence has been more far-reaching than anyone expected. One has only to mention a few of the many areas in which decisions were reached to realize the potential for profound future development in the Church : the rejection of the distinction between the clergy as leaders and the laity as those who are led, with the corollary that the laity should participate much more actively, not only in the Church's liturgy but in its whole life; the renewed emphasis put on freedom of conscience; the attention given to Scripture as revelation; the positive attitude not only towards other Christians but towards the non-Christian religions; the call for more action on the part of the Church in tackling the problems of society; and the involvement of all its bishops in the supreme government of the Church.

Sikhism provides an illustration of a completely different kind of reformation. It has had a permanent effect on the organization of the religion, but it did not cause a fundamental rethinking within the faith in the way that Vatican II has done. At the beginning of this century there was an attempt by the Sikhs in their homeland, the Punjab, to regain control of their gurdwaras (temples) from the *mahants*, a class of priests. Many of the *mahants* belonged to an order which was not within mainstream Sikhism, but they had so identified themselves with the gurdwaras that they personally appropriated the wealth of the temples. They exercised power in an arbitrary fashion and many of them were notorious for their corrupt and immoral lives. The British government in India, which had annexed the Punjab in the mid-nineteenth century, and brought the Sikh kingdom to an end, supported the *mahants*. Agitation continued and the British government, no doubt seeing it as a struggle for political independence, ruthlessly opposed the movement. The writer Khushwant Singh says that in the five years before the Sikhs won the right to control their gurdwaras when the Sikh Gurdwaras Act was eventually passed in 1925, 'over 30,000 men and women had gone to jail, nearly 400 had been killed and over 2,000 wounded'.[4] Ever since 1925 gurdwaras everywhere have been run by committees of elected representatives.

There have been a number of reform movements in Hinduism in the last 150 years. We shall take one of them as an illustration of the kind of reformation which is brought about by people who are outstanding individuals but who are not in positions of high authority in their religion.

The two men who were responsible for the Rāmakrishna Movement were very different from each other, and the contribution they made to the creation of the Movement was different. The actual organization of what is properly called the

[4] *The Sikhs Today* (Longmans Orient 1967), p. 61.

Rāmakrishna Math (i.e. Temple) and Mission was the work of Vivekānanda (1863–1902), a high caste intellectual, but the movement he founded in 1897 was based on the teachings of his master, the Bengali priest and mystic, Rāmakrishna (1836–86). The mystical experiences which Rāmakrishna had when he experimented for a period with Islam and Christianity convinced him of the basic unity of all religions underlying their varied manifestations. Rāmakrishna combined both the monistic (*advaita*) and the *bhakti* strands in Hinduism,[5] though the movement which bears his name has put much more emphasis on the former. As Swami Vivekānanda wrote, 'The ultimate goal of all mankind, the aim and end of all religions, is but one—reunion with God, or what amounts to the same, with the divinity which is every man's true nature.'[6]

Vivekānanda founded his monastic order on lines similar in many ways to those of the Christian Church. The monks (and the nuns in the women's order) do not marry, and they undertake medical and educational work and service to the poor and needy in India. The Mission now has centres in many countries and these have largely been responsible for the dissemination of knowledge about Hinduism outside India.

SCHISM

We have already had reason to note the divisions in religions (see pages 21f). Because faith involves commitment and because religions deal with ultimate questions, men have felt strongly about religious issues. Not all schismatic moves, of course, are motivated by high-mindedness, but the pages of history record many instances of men and women being prepared to die for what they believed to be the truth.

Schism occurs when one group cuts itself off from, or is cut off by, another group. It is not surprising, therefore, that schism occurs most frequently in religions like Christianity and Islam, which put such emphasis on orthodoxy. The numerous schools in Buddhism cannot be described as schismatic, and the term would be meaningless in Hinduism, where there is no centralized authority and no orthodox set of beliefs.

[5] See p. 62.
[6] Quoted in *Every Man His Own Sect* (Rāmakrishna Vedanta Centre, London), p. 8.

The rise of puritan movements sometimes leads to schism. This is familiar to us from post-Reformation Christian history, and it has also happened in Islam. The earliest of all the Islamic sects, the Khārijites, were men who led disciplined and ascetic lives. The undoubted admirable qualities of puritanism, however, all too often go with an unattractive moral zealousness and a fanatical selfrighteousness which create a separatist attitude. The Khārijites added *Jihād* (literally 'striving'), the doctrine of the religious war, to the five Pillars of Islam, and they thought nothing of killing fellow Muslims who did not live up to the standards they thought appropriate. A member of the Khārijite sect even assassinated Ali, the fourth Caliph.

It is not possible in such a brief compass to do justice to the complex nature of schisms. All kinds of factors—personality, historical situation, social conditions—play a part. If we are studying a schismatic group we must try to see it in its setting, and never just conclude that a disagreement about doctrine or morality was by itself the cause of the schism.

The major division in Christianity, known as the Great Schism, was between the Eastern and the Western sections of the Church. Its date is usually given as 1054, but this could mislead us if we did not know that tension had existed between the Eastern and Western Churches from the second century, particularly over the question of primacy; the Eastern Church, with its centre at Constantinople, rejected the claim of the Western, Latin, Church, that its chief bishop, the Pope of Rome, was the supreme authority in Christendom. Moreover, the ecclesiastical and doctrinal matters which brought about the final separation were debated for about two centuries before 1054, and continued to be debated for several centuries afterwards.

In brief treatments of the subject the cause of the Great Schism is usually given as the *filioque* clause in the Nicene creed. *Filioque* ('and from the Son') was not actually in the original draft of the creed agreed at the famous Council of Constantinople in 381, but the form of the creed which the Western Churches use begins the final paragraph with the words, 'And I believe in the Holy Ghost, the Lord and giver of life, who proceedeth from the Father and the Son'. The Eastern Church said that the Spirit proceeded from the Father *through* the Son. We need not go into the complex discussions about the doctrine of the Trinity. What is interesting for our purposes in the study of developments in religions is that although this and other causes of dissension which contributed to the Great Schism may well be removed in the foreseeable future, the Churches have developed apart for so long that there are now many other factors which make reunion difficult.

Because religions do not remain static, denominations and sects develop their own particular characteristics and emphases, which become so much an integral part of the faith that to be called on to sacrifice them can seem like having to sacrifice truth itself.

NEW RELIGIONS

This is a fascinating topic for anyone interested in the phenomenon of religion. What is it that from time to time causes a completely new religion to arise? Does it require particularly favourable circumstances, or would the religious genius of the founder have flowered whatever the circumstances?

There have been several periods in history which were particularly rich in religious movements. Not all of the movements resulted in the creation of new religions; nevertheless they made a significant contribution to the religious life of mankind.

One such period was the three hundred years from 800 to 500 B.C.E. In India a succession of remarkable men were composing the Upanishads and creating a school of philosophy which was to transform the Hinduism of the Vedas. In Israel the teaching of the great Hebrew prophets represented the culmination of Israel's theological development, and the experience of the exile in Babylon in the sixth century brought about the reshaping of the religion and laid the foundation for the development of Judaism as we know it today. During the sixth century two new religious movements, Buddhism and Jainism, appeared in north India. In Persia, Zarathushtra founded Zoroastrianism, and across in China the philosopher Confucius was teaching the ethical principles which came to be known as Confucianism.

Another striking period for religious development was the four hundred years which spanned the first two centuries B.C.E. and the first two centuries C.E. Christianity is the only religion which actually owes its origin to this period, but it was the age of the greatest development in Mahāyāna Buddhism. In Judaism it saw the rise of groups like the Pharisees and the Qumran community, and the flowering of the rabbinic schools which set the pattern for the direction Judaism was to take after the destruction of the Temple in 70 c.e. In China it witnessed the arrival of Buddhism, the establishment of Confucianism as an official cult, and the creation of Chang Ling, a Taoist sect which spread rapidly through the country.

The creation of new religions follows many different patterns. Some become universal religions, most remain relatively small cults. Some are founded intentionally, others develop out of what were originally reform movements. Some aim at reconciling existing religions but in the end succeed only in adding one more to the list.

It is instructive, however, to examine some of the features which new religions seem to have in common. First, they owe their origin to individuals. Foundations may have been laid by others, and there may be key men and women associated with the founder, but the founder himself (or, just occasionally, herself) is a charismatic leader, that is, someone endowed with natural authority and compelling personal qualities. He is recognized as possessing more than ordinary power, and is reverenced or even worshipped by his followers after his death, or sometimes even during his lifetime.

Secondly, the founders can be described as visionaries. Some of them actually have visionary experiences, as Muhammad did, in which they become aware of a new truth being revealed to them, but all are men of vision, 'seeing' further than their contemporaries. This experience of the givenness of the truth cannot always be described accurately as revelation, because that implies Someone who does the revealing. Gotama's enlightenment, which was the foundation experience of Buddhism, is more appropriately described as awareness or insight into the nature of reality.

Thirdly, new religions arise in reaction to some situation which is felt to be unsatisfactory. In many of the religions which have come into being in the twentieth century, economic and political frustration have obviously played an important part, but there is always a sense of dissatisfaction with the existing religion, either because it has reached a formalistic or decadent state, or because it no longer provides the answers to the questions men are asking. This is one of the reasons for the wide variation in the 'truth' which religions proclaim. The

78

founder is the product of one particular culture and religion, he is faced, as his contemporaries are, with the questions of that time and place, and his message is presented in terms of answers to those particular questions. It could not be otherwise. Buddhism therefore offered a way of liberation from the endless round of rebirths through one's own efforts; men no longer needed either to become ascetics or to be dependent on the Brahmin caste who controlled the sacrificial system of Hinduism and who alone had the 'knowledge' of salvation. To a people whose politico–religious hopes had been frustrated and who were acutely conscious of human sin, Christianity offered atonement for sin and a new life in the Messianic age which it claimed had at last dawned. To a polytheistic people who feared the power of the jinns and other spirits, Islam offered an uncompromising monotheism and a belief in the sovereignty of God over the whole of creation. To a society torn by communal strife, Sikhism offered a way of reconciliation.

Fourthly, however much a new religion rejects of the religion out of which it emerges, there is always some continuity. This may be from conscious choice. Neither Jesus nor the early Christians seem to have had any idea of rejecting Judaism as a religion. The God of Christianity was the God of Judaism; the scriptures of Christianity were the scriptures of Judaism. Far from renouncing his Jewish heritage in the way that Gotama sought to escape from the Hindu religion, Jesus not only acknowleged it but saw himself as part of its continuing development, and the first Christians proclaimed him as the inaugurator of the age which all Jews were looking for.

Continuity may be the result of an aspect of the existing religion being retained in the new one. The peoples of the Arabian peninsula worshipped Allāh as the supreme God among a host of gods and goddesses and spirits. Muhammad proclaimed that there was no God but Allāh, and that the greatest sin was to associate anyone with him. The Ka'ba (or Kaaba), the cube-shaped structure in Mecca, which is the focus of the Muslim pilgrimage and the centre to which all Muslims turn for prayer, was a pilgrimage shrine long before the time of Muhammad. Muslim tradition states that the present building was constructed by Abraham and Ishmael.

An interesting feature of new religions is the tendency in later

79

ages for their adherents to ignore the elements of continuity and to ascribe everything in their religion to the originality of the founder. Many Christians, for example, unaware of the character of first-century Judaism, assume that such things as teaching by parables, performing miracles of healing and exorcism, calling God 'Father', proclaiming the priority of inward sincerity over outward actions, and advocating the love of one's neighbour, are unique to Jesus.

There is always some form of continuity, even when it is not intended. As we noted above, the founder of a new religion is inevitably the product of a particular culture, and although he consciously rejects some aspects, there will be many others which he just takes for granted because they are in the air, so to speak. This is probably the case with Buddhism's belief in rebirth, which it shares with Hinduism, Jainism and Sikhism. 'Belief' is really the wrong word, because it is not an article of faith. It is just a 'fact' which has been taken as given in Indian thinking for more than two and a half thousand years.

It is, however, the combining of new ideas with those of the existing religion or culture which creates the main 'theological' problems for new religions. Buddhism, for example, inherited from Hinduism the doctrine of *karma*, the law of cause and effect which states that the conditions of one's life have been determined by one's actions and thoughts in previous lives, and it has had to wrestle with the problem of reconciling this with its new doctrine that there is no such thing as a permanent soul or self to be reborn. Similarly, Christianity has had to wrestle with the problem of reconciling the transcendent monotheism it inherited from Judaism with its new belief in God's immanence in a human life.

This tension is even more obvious in religions which are intentionally syncretistic, for example in Sikhism, which included elements from two completely different cultural traditions, Indian and Semitic. With Hinduism it shared the Indian concept of cyclic time, and the doctrines of *karma* and rebirth, but with Islam it shared an uncompromising monotheism and a horror of the use of images in worship.

The so-called new religions of Japan have also been syncretistic, but this is not surprising, for syncretism has been a feature of Japan's religious history as it has of China's. Shinto,

Buddhist, Tao, Confucian and, latterly, Christian elements have merged, not only in the formal creation of a sect or a cult, but in the thinking of ordinary people. What is distinctive about the 'new religions' is the speed with which they have developed. The earliest of them was founded about 150 years ago, but it is since the end of the Second World War that there has been such a remarkable increase in their numbers. It was estimated that by 1970 there were several hundred of them. Significant features of the post-war religions have been their tendency to reject the past and all that was associated with it, and the call for personal faith and devotion. That they spoke to a felt need in Japan has been shown by the way in which they have gained adherents, numbered in millions in some cases, though largely drawn from the less privileged sections of society.

It is interesting to compare the new religions of Japan with the cargo cults which have sprung up, apparently quite independently, in widely separated islands in Melanesia. A common feature of the cults is the belief that material goods will arrive by ship or by aeroplane. Of course there are many differences between the cargo cults and the Japanese religions, but we may notice the following characteristics. They are a twentieth-century phenomenon; the first cult dates from 1913, but there has been a rapid increase in their numbers since the Second World War. They are syncretistic, combining elements of their native traditions with elements drawn from the white man's culture—in this case technical and economic aspects. They demand a simple faith from their followers, and they look to the future for the solution of all problems. Their appeal is to people who are conscious of their lack of privilege in life. The anthropologist Cyril Belshaw has written:

> The new cult endeavors to copy significant European activities. There is the belief in shipping, that is, in the origin of cargoes—for remember, most Melanesians have not seen or experienced the manufacturing process. There is a mystical significance in the revolting white skin of Europeans, and in money, which he circulates so strangely; in flags and flag-poles, which the European treats with peculiar reverence; ... in soldiers and drilling—which *must* be mystical, for what use is there in it? ... These things supplied the modern elements

in the cargo myth, the myth which explained European successes and indicated the correct road to follow.[7]

The fact that developments like these are taking place in tribal religions is significant. The careful handing on of the traditional ways of doing things has been a strong feature of tribal society, as has the lack of interest in a golden age in the future. Once their comparative isolation is lost and they come into contact with other cultures, they cannot remain unaffected.

We have moved a long way from the creation of religions like Buddhism and Christianity and Islam, but the cargo cults of Melanesia present us with an example of religious development in a spectacular way, and they pose more sharply the question: by what criteria do we decide whether religious developments represent progress or decline?

[7] 'The Significance of Modern Cults in Melanesian Development', in W. A. Lessa and E. Z. Vogt, eds, *Reader in Comparative Religion* (Harper and Row 3rd edn 1972), p. 527.

8

WHERE DOES AUTHORITY LIE?

'Why don't all the religions unite and form one universal religion?' From time to time one hears this question being asked, when someone feels particularly frustrated by the things which divide men from each other.

The issues we have looked at so far in this book are enough to convince us of the unrealistic nature of the suggestion, but there is another factor which divides religions in such a way that even if they were to attempt to unite it would prove to be an insurmountable obstacle. The concept of authority is understood so differently, and the locus of authority varies so much, that there would be no common ground for deciding between those beliefs which belonged to the nature of ultimate truth and those which could be jettisoned for the sake of unity. Even those Christian denominations which agree in recognizing the authority of scripture in doctrinal matters have found it difficult enough to make such decisions. It is not just cynicism or faintheartedness which convinces us that it would be an impossible task for the varied faiths of mankind.

In this chapter we shall look at three of the main sources of authority in religions: the person and teaching of the founder, sacred writings, and the religious community.

FOUNDERS

Not all religions have historical founders. Hinduism and Shinto are two whose origins are lost in the mists of history. Primal religions often preserve memories in myth and legend of cult heroes, founders of the tribe. However, not only do they have no historical records but because all life is one for tribal peoples it would be meaningless to ask about the beginning of religion as such.

Where religions do owe their origin to a particular historical person, that person has a unique position within the faith. We

83

have already referred to the charismatic qualities of founders of religions (see page 78). They are men of vision, with the power to inspire others. They are teachers and communicators. It is the task of their successors to work out the implication of their teaching, and to integrate it into a coherent 'theological' system. However, no matter how great these successors are, or how creative they are as reformers of the faith, they are always subordinate to the founder.

The founder is usually believed to be a mediator of divine revelation. His teachings are preserved, at first orally and then in written form, and they carry final authority for his followers. But it is not only what he said that is authoritative, it is also how he lived. In some religions this is of paramount importance. Christians claim that Jesus showed us what man was meant to be. Their aim is to live Christ-like lives, and numerous books have been written in an attempt to explore the implications of following the example of Jesus in later ages and in completely different forms of society.

In the same way Muslims claim that Muhammad is the model of conduct and character for all men to follow. 'In his life-example one can seek guidance in all aspects of human life, from the highly personal to the purely social—as a man, a son, a husband, a father, a preacher, a teacher, a trader, a statesman, a commander, a peace-negotiator, a judge or a head of state.'[1] The information in the Qur'ān about Muhammad's life is limited, so it is supplemented by the Hadīth, a vast collection of sayings and accounts of incidents which illustrate the Prophet's character.

We can find a common core of ethical precepts in the teaching of most of the founders of religions—commands about compassion, sincerity, honesty, love of one's neighbour, etc.—but there is considerable variation in the ways in which religions regard the person of their founder. In many of the new religions, especially those of Japan, the founder is believed by his (or her) followers to be divine or at least semi-divine, but this is not the case with most of the older established religions. Sikhism is emphatic that Guru Nanak was not God, or God incarnate. He is described as someone whose search for the truth led him to the conviction that all men were one, and that the practices

[1] Khurshid Ahmad, *Family Life in Islam* (The Islamic Foundation, Leicester 1974), p. 11.

of Hinduism and Islam were obstacles to man's union with God. He began his mission with the proclamation that there was no Hindu and no Muslim. He is seen by his followers as a teacher and as a godly man, and many of his hymns and prayers are included in the Granth, the Sikh scriptures, but his person does not dominate the religion.

Muslims deny vehemently that Muhammad was divine, but he has a much more dominant role in Islam than Guru Nanak has in Sikhism. Muslims believe that he was the supreme Prophet, the Messenger through whom God revealed his will for all mankind, and because he was the bearer of the very words of God, his authority is unsurpassed.

In the first two or three centuries of the Muslim era there were certain developments which accorded a more than human status to Muhammad. A doctrine of his sinlessness was developed. Many miracles were attributed to him, and one of the great Sūfī prayers even speaks of his eternal existence. However, Muslims have always maintained that worship belonged to God alone.

Much of Christian theology has been concerned with the problem created by the Christian insistence that Jesus was fully human but that he was also the incarnation of God. What is distinctive of the Christian faith is not Jesus' ethical teaching, which has much in common with the ethical teaching of the Jewish rabbis of his time, but the belief that he was the final revelation to man of the nature of God, and that through his identification with man, and his perfect obedience, he wrought man's salvation. The authority of the person of Jesus for Christians is therefore not the authority of an inspired teacher, or even the authority of a person through whom God made his will known; it cannot be entirely separated from the authority of God himself. For Christians Jesus is not only the communicator of the faith he founded; he is part of the content of the faith itself.

The role of Gotama in Buddhism is different again. Theravāda Buddhists emphasize that he was a human being who found the way to enlightenment and taught that way to others, and that he never made any claim to divinity. The stories which are told about his previous lives do not, of course, indicate any supernatural status for the Buddha. In Buddhist belief everyone has had countless previous lives, but the Buddha is able to remember

85

his whereas most people have no memory of their former existences.

The development of buddhology, that is, beliefs about the Buddha, has been one of the characteristics of Mahāyāna Buddhism. Gotama, the historical Buddha, became less and less important. Not only were characteristics of divinity ascribed to the Buddha, with the accompanying *bhakti* cult, but there developed a belief in a large number of mythical Buddhas. One of these was Amitabha (Amida in Japanese), the Buddha of Infinite Light, who became the object of worship in the Pure Land Sect. It is not meaningful, therefore, to speak of the authority of the founder of the religion in Mahāyāna Buddhism, and even in the Theravāda school it is the Dharma of the Buddha—his teaching—which has authority rather than his person.

SACRED WRITINGS

We have had reason to refer to scriptures and other sacred writings a number of times in previous chapters. They play an important part in practically every religion, but their nature and their authority vary widely.

At one end of the spectrum is the Muslim attitude to the Qur'ān. As we have seen, Muslims believe that it contains the very words of God, which were received by Muhammad in a series of revelations. It is called the Word of God, and it is treated with the utmost reverence. This reverence is shown outwardly: no other book may be placed on top of the Qur'ān, a person must wash before reading it, it must be listened to in silence, and no one may eat, drink or smoke while it is being read. The outward actions reflect the Muslim's attitude towards the contents of the Qur'ān. For orthodox adherents of the faith there can be no questioning of any of its statements, from the narratives about earlier prophets such as Abraham and Moses and Jesus to descriptions of the attributes of God, from laws governing the running of the state to prescriptions for the dividing of a family inheritance. It would be misleading to think of the Qur'ān as the equivalent of the Bible in Christianity. Its place in Islam is more akin to the place of Christ in Christianity.

Outside the scriptures, but still carrying authority for Muslims, is the Hadīth, or Tradition of the Prophet. The number of separate *hadīths* has been estimated as hundreds of thousands. Not all of them are genuine sayings of the Prophet or stories about him, but such importance is attached to the person of Muhammad that in the early centuries of Islamic history scholars developed the science of *hadīth*-criticism, and devoted their lives to tracing the chain of authorities through which each *hadīth* had been passed on. Only those were accepted as genuine which could be traced back either to Muhammad himself or to one of the Companions (i.e. men who became Muslims during Muhammad's lifetime).

Like Islam, Judaism has two categories of sacred writings, the Bible and the Talmud, but in many ways they provide a striking contrast to the Qur'ān and the Hadīth. The Qur'ān took its final written form within twenty years of Muhammad's death, but the Jewish Bible includes material from a period of nearly a thousand years, and the Talmud is the result of many hundreds of years of rabbinic scholarship. It is most important to Islam that, humanly speaking, the Qur'ān owes its origin entirely to Muhammad, and the Hadīth is nothing but traditions about Muhammad, but the Jewish sacred writings owe their origin to a large number of people, and they include many different types of literature.

The question of the authority of Judaism's sacred writings is also much more complex. Within the Bible itself there are distinctions. Of its three divisions, the ascending order of authority is: Writings, Prophets, Torah.[2] The Torah, the first five books of the Bible, is the basis of Judaism's life, and the standard by which everything else is judged. Readings from the Torah form the main part of synagogue worship, and its centrality in the religion is symbolized by the festival of Simchat Torah—Rejoicing of the Law. This takes place in the synagogue on the ninth and last day of the Feast of Tabernacles, and it marks the end of the cycle of the reading of the Torah. Men carrying the scroll of the Law lead a joyous procession of children with banners, and children are called up for the reading of the Law. Then the last part of Deuteronomy is read, and immediately, to emphasize the fact that the reading of Torah is continuous, the first part of Genesis.

However, when a Jew wants to know how he should order his life, he is more likely to go to the Talmud than to the Bible.

[2] See p. 43.

87

Talmud is short for Talmud Torah, meaning 'study of the Law', and it represents the end product of centuries of development of the Oral Law. It is a vast collection of material, partly Halakhah (literally 'walking')—legal teaching and practice—and partly Aggadah (literally 'narrative')—religious and ethical teachings, often in the form of stories and parables. To describe the Talmud as authoritative could give a misleading impression of its character. It is certainly not authoritarian. One rabbi said : 'When Torah came into the world freedom came into the world.' A codification of the Law, such as the Mishnah,[3] does not present Jews with a monolithic legal system. Rather it provides a basis for further study. It is in many ways a record of discussions; variant judgements given by different rabbis are included, and it does not arbitrate among them. Every rabbinic judgement is ultimately based on the Mosaic Law, but it is an application of the original Law to meet new situations.

The work of interpreting the Law of Moses did not come to an end with the completion of the Talmud. It is a never-ending task because the Law is about obedience in everyday living, and this means applying it in ever changing conditions. A modern illustration of this continuing process is the recently published book by Rabbi Louis Jacobs. It is called *What does Judaism say about ... ?*[4] The first five of the 109 topics it deals with are : Abortion, Adoption, Advertising, Aged, Care of, and Alcohol, and the last five are : Vegetarianism, Welfare State, Women's Liberation, Work, and Zen.

The role of sacred writings in the Indian religious traditions is completely different from their role in Islam or Judaism. Both Hinduism and Buddhism have a vast number of writings, and many of them expound the teachings of the religions, but, apart from the Vinaya Pitaka, that is, the section of the Buddhist Pali Canon which deals with monastic discipline, they do not include detailed legislation regulating the way people live. The fact that Mahāyāna Buddhism has been based on the concept of developing doctrine has meant that no writings could be regarded as having ultimate authority, though a sect may choose a particular Sūtra (a collection of sayings ascribed to the Buddha) as its basic text.

One of the Mahāyāna schools, however, stands alone in

[3] See p. 39.
[4] Keter Publishing House 1973.

rejecting the authority of any text. The attitude of Zen Buddhism is summed up in the words:

> A special transmission outside Scripture.
> No reliance on words.
> Direct pointing at the heart of man.
> Seeing your nature and becoming a Buddha.

Hinduism has two categories of sacred writings: *sruti* and *smriti*. *Sruti* means 'heard', though it refers not to the normal process of hearing but to the hearing of cosmic truths by sages at the beginning of a world cycle.[5] *Sruti* comprises the Veda (literally 'knowledge'), a body of several different kinds of literature, including the Rig-Vedas and the Upanishads. The latter are known as the Vedānta, or 'end of the Veda'. The literature of the Veda, which is technically the scriptures of Hinduism, was written over a period of about a thousand years.

Smriti means 'remembered', that is, handed on from generation to generation. It comprises an innumerable number of writings, and it has no clearly defined boundaries, merging with the popular stories and folk tales of India. Hindu scholars are versed in the literature of the Veda, but it is the myths and stories of the Purānas and the epics, the Mahābhārata and the Rāmāyana, which are known and loved by ordinary people. Different individuals and different sects in Hinduism respond to particular writings which thereby acquire an authority for them, but this is an accepted and never an imposed authority.

Sikhism's sacred writings are quite different from those of the other Indian religions. Its scriptures, the Granth, contain about six thousand hymns, composed mainly by Guru Nanak and five of the other early Gurus, but including also a number which were written by Hindu and Muslim saints. The tenth Guru, Gobind Singh, who was responsible for the final compilation of the Granth, declared that it would be the eleventh and continuing teacher of the community, the Guru to whom Sikhs would look for guidance. It is therefore called Guru Granth Sahib, and treated with the kind of respect which would be shown to the most honoured person. In the gurdwara it is placed on cushions on a platform, under a canopy, and the *granthi* (reader) waves over it the *chauri*, or whisk, which is part of the insignia of authority and status.

[5] See pp. 51f.

89

Although the Granth is devotional in character and does not include expository teaching or legislation, it has supreme authority in Sikhism. Not only are its hymns a source of inspiration and guidance to Sikhs, but its role is crucial in every aspect of the religion. It is in the presence of the Guru Granth Sahib that every ceremony takes place, whether it is the naming of a baby, or a marriage, or the Amrit (baptism) ritual.

What is the authority of the scriptures in Christianity? As we have seen, much the largest part of the Bible happens to be also the Bible of Judaism. What, then, is the authority of the Old Testament for Christians? Christians call their Bible the Word of God. If this is not the 'words' of God, as in Islam, what does it mean? Christianity, like Judaism and Islam has 'revealed' scriptures, but Christians are divided not only about the degree of authority the scriptures should have, but about how they should be interpreted. They range from extreme literalists at one end of the spectrum to extreme liberals at the other, and the whole range of approaches is represented within most of the Churches.[6]

THE RELIGIOUS COMMUNITY

To be an adherent of a religion is to belong to a religious tradition, but what does belonging involve?

Some religions are highly structured, with a pattern of corporate activities for their members, from congregational worship to groups for study, recreation and voluntary service. The two obvious examples are Judaism and Christianity. One of the consequences of this kind of structured organization is that there are recognizable levels of membership. There is the 'inner circle', the dedicated members whose commitment both to the faith and to the organized community is never in doubt. Then there is the larger number of people, whose names appear on the membership rolls and who are reasonably faithful attenders, but whose part in the various activities is more likely to be a passive one. After this, distinctions get a bit blurred as we move from the people who attend services of worship when there are no other competing interests to those who turn up once a year,

[6] The question of the authority of scripture for Christians is treated fully in one of the other books in this series, David Stacey, *Interpreting the Bible*. Sheldon Press 1976.

at Christmas or Yom Kippur (Day of Atonement).

This concept of membership does not exist in a religion like Hinduism. Worship is an individual matter. The Hindu family will almost certainly have a shrine at home; families who can afford it set aside a room, but the humblest home will have a shelf or a table with pictures of particular deities, flowers, and vessels for the daily offering of *pūjā* (prayers).

In India throughout every day there will be people visiting the temples to make their own private offering of worship.[7] Some Hindus regularly visit one particular temple, others may visit several. How and when one worships is purely a matter of individual choice, and there are no clear-cut boundaries between the different 'sects'. When a Methodist goes to a Greek Orthodox church or an Anglican to a Baptist church he is very conscious of having stepped outside his own denomination, and of being a visitor, but many Shaivite Hindus would not feel so strange in a temple dedicated to Vishnu.

This contrast in structure reflects a contrast in the nature of the community's authority. To be a 'member' of one of the more structured religions imposes certain obligations, of belief or practice or both, and is normally marked by a ceremony at which the obligations are formally accepted. Sometimes there is a particular ceremony for those who have grown up in the religion, such as Judaism's Bar Mitzvah, but in other religions, for example in Sikhism and Christianity, the ceremony is the same for converts to the faith as for those who have grown up in it.

Islam is an interesting exception to what we have said in the last paragraph. In spite of being a faith which demands a very disciplined response from its adherents, it has no procedure for 'joining' the religion. If one submits to God one is a Muslim. This submission, which involves accepting the basic beliefs and the five Pillars of Islam, has to be made by each person; anyone who no longer submits is no longer 'muslim'.

[7] Hindus who live in countries like Britain do not have the same opportunities for practising their religion as they would have in India, and their religious life is likely to approximate more to that of the structured religions. They will meet for worship, and perhaps for a communal meal (usually on Sundays because then people are free from work), partly because it is not possible to keep temples open and staffed continuously and partly because a sense of community is essential for a minority group in an alien culture.

It is perhaps not surprising that the more highly structured religions make more careful provision for the instruction of their adherents, through sermons, through literature, and particularly through the education of children, though the way in which children are nurtured in the faith varies considerably. In Islam the process starts at birth. The new-born baby has the call to prayer[8] whispered first into his right ear and then into his left ear, symbolizing the fact that there is no moment in his life when he is not aware of religious truth. When he is about four years old he starts to learn to read the Qur'ān and to recite long passages from memory. For Muslims who are not also Arabs this means learning Arabic, because Arabic is the only language used for the Qur'ān. Children learn the meaning of the Arabic text, but they will read and recite the scriptures only in the original language. Muslim children also have to master a sizeable body of knowledge about the life of Muhammad and the teachings of the faith.

Judaism lays much more stress on how its members live than on what they believe. Children are not instructed in beliefs. The Shema, 'Hear, O Israel: the Lord our God, the Lord is One' (Deut. 6.4) is recited several times a day, and this basic belief is therefore an ever-present part of a Jewish child's life, but he is not given systematic instruction in the faith. Rather, he grows up in a religious family. The focus of Judaism is the home, and it is here that the child learns, not by precept but by example, and not just by watching but by participating. The part played by children in the routine observances in the home, at the synagogue, and in the festivals is much greater than in any other religion.

In the Indian religions children also learn through being part of a family. They hear readings from the Purānas, they see dramas performed, and they take part in all the festivals, but this is mainly because the family is a natural unit and children are not excluded from it rather than because a special part has been 'written in' for them as it has been in Judaism.

In the teaching of adults it is the role of the personal teacher, the guru, in a religion like Hinduism, which provides the most striking contrast between the Western religions and the less

[8] 'Allah is greatest. There is no God but Allah. Muhammad is the Prophet of Allah. Hasten to prayer. Hasten to success. Allah is greatest. There is no God but Allah.'

structured faiths. A guru is not a teacher in the sense in which we use the word. He is a spiritual master, and it is a spiritual search, not an intellectual one, which leads a man to attach himself to a guru. Even being in the presence of a spiritual master contributes in an indefinable way to the disciple's spiritual pilgrimage, and the relationship with the guru is more important than his actual teaching. A guru is regarded as a mediator of the divine, and he represents for his disciples the supreme religious authority.

Most but certainly not all religions have a professional class responsible for the conduct of worship. As we have seen, this is not necessarily congregational worship. Shinto priests, for example, are responsible for the upkeep of the temples and for the maintenance of the ceremonies. They offer regular worship to the *kami* (deities), and perform the traditional rites, many of them concerned with the removal of ritual pollution. Hindu priests, who are drawn mainly from the Brahmin caste, are also responsible for the regular worship of the temples, but they are much more involved in the life of the ordinary worshipper, especially through the rites of passage.[9] They will go to the home of the bride, for instance, to perform the appropriate rituals at the marriage ceremony.

Islam, on the other hand, has no priesthood. Although the Arabic word *imām* is sometimes translated as 'priest' it really means 'leader'. An *imām*[10] is the person who leads the prayers, and although many mosques do have a permanent *imām*, any respected male member of the Muslim community can act as leader.

Judaism similarly has no priesthood. It does have ordained professionals, rabbis, but they are people who are learned in the Law, and their main function in the community is the continued study and interpretation of Torah. Most synagogues have a rabbi who acts as minister to the congregation, and who may well carry the main responsibility for the conduct of worship, but this is not necessary; worship can be led by any competent layman.

Since 1925 Sikhism has had no priests (see page 74). Much of Sikh worship consists of readings from the Granth, and the

[9] See p. 14.
[10] Except in the Shi'ite sects, where the supreme leader of the sect is called the Imām.

granthi (reader) will be a person who is respected in the community for his piety and his knowledge of the faith. A *granthi* may be a man or a woman.

The Christian Churches differ almost as much within Christianity as the religions do from each other, ranging from those with the three-fold order of bishops, priests and deacons at one end of the scale to groups, such as the Society of Friends, with no ordained ministry whatsoever. Christianity combines the responsibility for both teaching and the conduct of worship to an extent not found in many other religions, and preparation for the ministry involves training for leadership in both areas. This centralizes authority, particularly at the local level, in one person much more than is the case in Judaism or Islam. In Orthodox Judaism especially there are many laymen who are advanced Torah students, so that there is no sharp distinction between the rabbi and the learned members of the congregation.

Although there are no 'clergy' in Islam, there is a professional class, the *Ulamā* (literally 'learned men'). They are the guardians of orthodoxy and, because the faith includes not only the Muslim's 'religious' obligations but a great deal of legislation which in other societies would be called civil law, their authority is extensive. They control the interpretation of both law and theology. They teach in the *madrasas*, or Muslim institutions of higher education, and are the defenders of Islam against the corroding effects of contact with the Western world or of modernist movements within Islam itself. There are a number of groups which do not recognize the authority of mainstream Islam. For example, the Sūfī orders have always placed more emphasis on personal experience and devotion to God than on the observance of 'religious' and legal obligations, and the Ahmadiyya, a missionary-minded sect founded in North India towards the end of the nineteenth century, is much less traditionalist in its approach than Sunni Islam, and it does not consider itself bound by the decisions of the *Ulamā*.

Heresy is a concept which can have meaning only in religions like Islam and Christianity, where considerable emphasis is put on what a person believes, and the history of both these religions records many battles for the preservation of the orthodox faith. This raises the question: What is orthodoxy? Has it anything to do with numbers, like democracy? Are the majority right and the minority wrong? And how do the adherents of a religion

94

distinguish between a heresy and an important new insight into the truth? This has been no mere academic question for many Roman Catholics in the mid-seventies. The French archbishop who accused the Pope of being a heretic claimed that he and his supporters were upholding the orthodox faith of the Church by rejecting the changes which followed the second Vatican Council.

As we noted earlier, no group is prepared to accept the label 'heretical'. In religion more than in any other area of life men care deeply and passionately about truth. A number of religions (or sometimes sects within those religions) believe that they alone have the full truth; others are prepared to acknowledge truth in other faiths, but no man would be an adherent of a religion if he believed that its teachings were false. They have ultimate authority for him even when he is willing to grant that the teachings of other religions rightly have ultimate authority for other men.

Part 3

QUESTIONS OF TRUTH

9

MAKING JUDGEMENTS

The study of religions is, ideally, an objective activity. We stand back from all religions, even our own. We suspend judgement about the truth of religions because we are trying to understand how they represent truth to their adherents. This does not mean that our study is cold and detached, as if we were dissecting specimens on a laboratory bench. After all, we are doing this study because, at the very least, we think that religion is not only interesting but somehow important. Even if we do not stand firmly within a religious tradition ourselves we become aware that for hundreds of millions of people in the world religion is not something you study but something you live, something which makes a coherent pattern of your life—your hopes and your fears, your highest ideals and your awareness of your own limitations, your questions about the meaning of life and, at an even more profound level, your questions about death. Such people do not *decide* to be religious, as one might decide to take up stamp collecting or sailing; they *are* religious, and their religion has to do with the deepest things of life. One of the aims of our study is to learn what religious commitment means to religious people, and we therefore have to try to understand their emotional commitment as well as their intellectual beliefs and their practices.

We are attempting to discover why a religion satisfies the deepest needs of its adherents. Whether we think it would satisfy us is quite a different issue. The purpose of the study of religions is not so that we may choose one for ourselves. It will have become obvious long before this that one doesn't just choose a religion as one chooses a product displayed on the shelves of a supermarket. Religions involve not only certain beliefs and practices but a whole way of understanding the world, with its distinctive language and thought-forms and its cultural heritage. This does not preclude us from having feelings, positive or negative, about particular religions. It would be strange indeed if we did not respond more warmly to some than to others. What we must avoid is prejudging, making judgements on the basis of very limited knowledge.

We are, however, confronted in our study with more profound issues than our own personal reactions. Religions make claims to truth. What should our approach be in this area? Do we just say that Buddhism is true for the Buddhist and that Christianity is true for the Christian? This is not what the religions themselves say. They make claims about the nature of ultimate reality; they say that *this* is what the world is like, and *this* is what man's life is for. At least some of these claims cannot be reconciled with each other. Either there is a personal God or there isn't. Either man has one life on this earth or he has many lives. How does one set about making any serious judgements about religions?

PRESUPPOSITIONS

The first and most important fact to recognize is that there is no neutral ground from which to make such judgements. Our particular way of understanding the world and our values have been shaped by the culture in which we have grown up.

It is true that one can reject the values of one's own culture. In the sixties thousands of young people in Europe and America rejected the values of their society. However, what they turned their backs on were such things as competitiveness, hypocrisy, intellectualism, racial and national conflict, and the treating of property as more sacred than persons. Many of them rejected Christianity because they identified it with their society, but ironically the values they used as criteria for judging that society, were basically the values of the Christian faith which they had absorbed, consciously or unconsciously, from the culture to which they belonged.

The fact that we are inescapably part of what we are trying to evaluate meets us whichever way we turn. Some Christian philosophers of religion have suggested that one criterion we might apply in comparing the truth claims of religions is the inner coherence of their belief system. However, although Western philosophy values coherence, the criterion

98

does not do justice to a religion like Hinduism. To a Hindu, truth is not something which can be neatly encapsulated in a tidy system. As we saw in Chapter 5, what might be thought of as contradictions in Western religions—good and evil, creation and destruction, asceticism and sensuality—are held together in Indian thought as essential and complementary, and sometimes paradoxical, parts of the whole.

Again, it has been suggested that even though one could hardly test the truth of a religion's beliefs about the nature of the deity, one could compare beliefs about the nature of man. When this criterion is applied some Christian thinkers have come to the conclusion that Christianity's understanding of man is superior to that of other religions because of the significance it gives to persons. It is not surprising that they come to this conclusion, for this is also their starting point. They take with them to the task of evaluation this central Christian principle. A Buddhist on the other hand, armed equally with a central principle of his religion, would say that it is in the understanding of persons that Christianity has the least claim to truth. Salvation for the Buddhist comes only when we recognize that there *is* no such thing as a real self, that belief in the existence of the self is only an illusion to which we cling and from which we must be freed.

We have referred in earlier chapters to the assumptions made by nineteenth-century scholars both in anthropology and in the study of religions. They applied the concept of evolution, borrowed from biology, in the study of religion just as it was being applied in ethics and economics and politics. It was taken for granted that development moves naturally in an upward direction, from lower to higher forms. One popular theory, for example, suggested that the earliest stage of religion was animism, which gradually developed into polytheism, and that eventually produced monotheism. The famous anthropologist, Sir James Frazer, suggested that religion itself had developed out of magic, and would in turn be superseded by science. Such theories are, of course, no longer taken seriously. E. E. Evans-Pritchard, writing about the theories put forward to account for primitive man's beliefs and for the origin and development of religion, said: 'To comprehend what now seem to be obviously faulty interpretations and explanations, we would have to write a treatise on the climate of thought of their time, the intellectual circumstances which set bounds to their thought, a curious mixture of positivism, evolutionism, and the remains of a sentimental religiosity.'[1]

When we look back at the writings of the nineteenth-century scholars it is easy to see how their work was influenced by their presuppositions. But we have no cause to feel superior. We are just as much the product of our age and intellectual climate as they were of theirs. What are the current philosophies of the twentieth century? What do we believe about the nature of man? Behaviourist psychology proceeds on the basis of certain assumptions no less than Freudian psychology. The electronics age influences our thinking just as much as the industrial age and the discoveries of geology and biology influenced the thinking of our Victorian forbears.

A person's individual presuppositions can also affect the judgements he makes. It is not without significance that most of the nineteenth-century theories which suggested that the origin of religion lay in man's projection of his fears, or his mistaken ideas about natural phenomena, or some other misreading of his world, came from men who were either atheists or agnostics. They were not so much explaining religion as explaining it away. (We might ponder the fact that some Christians have tried similarly to 'explain away' other religions.)

It is sometimes claimed that religious people are not the best people to study or teach religion because they have a vested interest in it. But there is no neutral position here, just as there is no neutral position for comparing religions. The religious person has certain presuppositions about the value and truth of religion; the non-religious person also has certain presuppositions about the value and truth of religion. We have used the expression 'non-religious person' rather than the more common 'non-believer', because in the realm of ultimate questions there is no such thing as a non-believer. The atheist believes that there is no God; he believes that there is no life after death. He is no more able to produce proof of his negative beliefs than the religious person is able to produce proofs of his positive ones.

One of the characteristics of religious studies is that it attracts both religious and non-religious students. Does one of these

[1] *Theories of Primitive Religion* (O.U.P. 1965), p. 5.

groups have an advantage over the other? Does an atheist's natural scepticism help him to be more objective, or might his 'certainty' that there is no transcendental reality make it difficult for him to understand the nature of religion? Does a religious person's faith help him to understand commitment in other religions, or might it prevent him from treating 'rival' faiths seriously? No doubt these questions will continue to be debated, but one thing is certain: none of us approaches the study of religions without presuppositions of one kind or another. However, if we are sensitive and imaginative in our study, we shall be able to move away from any *fixed* presuppositions, and we shall be less dogmatic in rejecting judgements which differ from our own.

CHRISTIAN THEOLOGY OF RELIGIONS

During the last century, with the greatly increased contact between nations, the religions of the world have had to come to terms with the existence of other religions in a completely new way. There are still some sects and some individuals who reject all religions except their own as totally false, but this is not the official position of any one of the major religions.

All religions recognize at least partial truth in other faiths. It would be virtually impossible to do otherwise. For example, Christianity shares with Judaism and Islam the beliefs that there is only one God, that he is the creator of the universe, and that he is personal. At the very least, therefore, Christianity could not reject these Jewish and Muslim beliefs as false. Similarly, Islam gives qualified approval to Judaism and Christianity because they are also 'religions of the Book'.

In this section we are looking specifically at the Christian approach to a theology of religions, partly because it is likely to be of more immediate relevance to an English language readership and partly because the absoluteness of Christian claims makes the co-existence of other faiths a more acute problem for Christianity than it does for many other religions.

The Gospel which the first Christians proclaimed was not the announcement of a programme of ethical teaching by which man should live, nor even the offer of a means of salvation for individuals; rather it was the proclamation that God had acted decisively in history, that in Jesus Christ he had inaugurated a new age, and that this event had cosmic significance. It is the

101

'scandal of particularity', the fact that the Christian faith rests on a particular event, which took place at a particular time in history, and at a particular place on the map, rather than on timeless truths, which makes the truth claims of other religions such a thorny problem. If the Christ event is God's final, or unique, revelation to man, how are other religions to be interpreted?

The attempt at interpretation is not new. In the second century the task was undertaken by scholars who are called Apologists, because they sought to justify the reasonableness of the Christian faith to its opponents in the pagan world. These opponents were Greek intellectuals, and one of the main arguments of the Apologists was based on the Greek concept of the Logos, or Word, the principle of reason underlying the universe, and present in every man. The Apologists said that the Logos was the agent of God's revelation to man. The Logos had appeared to the Old Testament patriarchs and inspired the prophets and, in the fullness of time, had become incarnate in the person of Jesus. However, because a seed or germ of the Logos was in every man, every man could, if he developed that seed, live 'according to reason'. Justin Martyr, the first great Apologist, even went so far as to call some of the pagan philosophers and some of the men of the Old Testament 'Christians before Christ'.

Although the Apologists couched their arguments largely in terms of Greek philosophy (not surprisingly, as they were trying to communicate with Greek philosophers), these arguments were not without biblical foundation.

In the biblical doctrine of creation, *all* men are made in the image of God; it is by virtue of his humanity that man has the breath of God breathed into him, not by virtue of his adherence to a particular faith. In the story of Noah God entered into a covenant with the whole of mankind (Gen. 9.8–17). Turning to literature written many centuries later, we find Paul declaring, in his letter to the Romans, that God's revelation had not been confined to the Jews. The Gentiles too had had an opportunity to know God. 'For all that may be known of God by men lies plain before their eyes; indeed God himself has disclosed it to them.' (Rom. 1.19) And Acts gives us the famous speech on Mars Hill, in which Paul tells the Athenians that the Unknown God they worship is the God he is proclaiming. This is the God who 'created the world and everything in it ... He created every race of men of one stock ... They were to seek God, and, it might be, touch and find him; though indeed he is not far from each one of us, for in him we live and move, in him we exist.' (Acts 17.24–7)

The concept of the Logos is used by the author of the fourth Gospel in his prologue (John 1.1–14). John says that through the Word (Greek *logos*), who was with God at the beginning, 'all things came to be; no single thing was created without him. All that came to be was alive with his life, and that life was the light of men'.

The idea that it is possible for non-Christians to be saved if they live up to the highest that they know has been explored by a number of theologians in the twentieth century. It has been suggested, for example, that such people belong to the 'invisible' Church, or that they are 'anonymous' Christians, or that the non-Christian religions are the 'ordinary' way of salvation, while the Christian faith is the 'extraordinary' way of salvation.

Most of the theologians who have attempted to solve the problem along these lines have been members of the Roman Catholic Church, a Church which through history has taken a very definite stand: *extra ecclesiam nulla salus* (no salvation outside the Church). However, not only have many of the individuals who have been in the forefront of positive thinking about other religions in both theology and dialogue been Roman Catholics, but the Second Vatican Council produced a declaration on non-Christian religions which recognized that God's grace can work through other religions to fulfil his saving purpose, and that it is possible for men to be saved *within* their religions, which 'reflect a ray of that Truth which enlightens every man'.

Once it has been allowed that men can be saved through non-Christian religions, the question arises: What, then, is the uniqueness which Christians claim for God's saving act in Christ?

The missionary activity of the Church was motivated mainly by the conviction that without the Gospel men would perish eternally. Both the ignorance of other religions and the concern for the eternal fate of their adherents are illustrated by this extract from a book which was written just before the great missionary age which began at the end of the eighteenth century, and which was widely used as a source book for the Victorian surveys of religion. Writing of Hinduism, William Hurd said:

> As there are different sects among the Brahmins in religion, so they have six sects of philosophers, and one of these is considered in the same manner as we do Atheists. They have no skill in anatomy, and as to their tables of astronomy and chronology, they are not worth mentioning. When the moon is eclipsed, they believe she is fighting with a black ugly devil. They imagine the night is created by the sun's withdrawing himself behind a mountain, where he retires to rest, and in the morning makes his appearance.
>
> Such is the religion of the principal tribes who form the vast empire of the Great Mogul, and when we consider the deplorable state to which they are reduced, with respect to the knowledge of the true God, it must fill us with sorrow to reflect, that so many of our fellow creatures are still unacquainted with the Gospel ... It is long since we have had settlements in different parts of the East-Indies, but our merchants have been too intent in acquiring immense fortunes to use any means towards promoting the salvation of thousands of immortal souls, who are still sitting in darkness, and in the region and shadow of death.[2]

Although it was concern for the eternal fate of non-Christians which sent dedicated men and women out to the ends of the earth, it was eventually from the so-called mission field that new theological thinking about other religions developed. It was here, of course, that the problem was focused most sharply. Missionaries had the opportunity to gain a truer picture of the religions than the stereotype which was generally held by Christians. They also got to know devout adherents of those religions, men and women whose spiritual qualities were undeniable, and whose lives reflected the 'love, joy, peace, patience, kindness, goodness, fidelity, gentleness, and self-control' which Paul had called the 'harvest of the Spirit' (Gal. 5.22).

It would be quite wrong to suggest that all missionaries held the same views about the non-Christian religions. Even today, especially in the non-denominational missionary societies, many

[2] *A New and Universal History of the Religious Rites, Ceremonies and Customs of the Whole World* (London, n.d.), p. 57.

missionaries believe that a convert to the Christian faith must make a complete break with his 'old' religion, that there is no part of it which can contribute to his spiritual development as a Christian. However, much of the ferment of thinking about the Christian theology of religions has taken place in missionary circles.

One of the most important figures in this debate was Hendrik Kraemer, who in 1922 went out to Indonesia with the Dutch Bible Society to work among Muslims. Sixteen years later he wrote the preparatory volume for the international missionary conference at Tambaram in South India. His book was called *The Christian Message in a Non-Christian World*,[3] and the issues it raised dominated not only the Tambaram conference in 1938 but the whole debate in the following quarter of a century. Kraemer distinguished between the religions, as human attempts to reach God, and God's revelation to man in Christ.

This distinction had been made, even more sharply, by the great Swiss theologian, Karl Barth. Barth had been highly critical of the report of the previous international missionary conference at Jerusalem in 1928, which saw the non-Christian religions as partners in the task of stemming the rising tide of secularism in the world. Barth said that the Gospel had nothing to do with religion. He contrasted reason and revelation. Man could have no knowledge of God except as it was revealed through Christ. Human attempts to know God could achieve nothing. In fact, all religions, including the Christian religion, were obstacles to faith.[4]

By the time Kraemer wrote *Religion and the Christian Faith*[5] in 1956 he had moved his position slightly. He allowed that there might be some indications of God's revelation in non-Christian religions. However, his main argument, that there can be no co-operation with other religions, remained the same, and together the two volumes stand as the classic expression of an approach which is scholarly and sensitive, and yet firm in its rejection of any continuity between the Christian faith and the non-Christian religions.

One of the difficulties of the neo-orthodox approach, with its

[3] Edinburgh House Press.
[4] The school of thought which is based on Barth's theological position called 'neo-orthodoxy'.
[5] Lutterworth Press.

emphasis on the distinction between the Gospel and religion, including the Christian religion, is how one can separate the revelation from the religion. The Word of God does not exist in a vacuum. Far from being a disembodied revelation, it is 'embodied' in the way of life and the thought forms of the culture in which it is received, and man's response of faith is to a God whose nature and attributes are understood in terms of a particular religion. To take an extreme example, the Christian has always thought of God as male, because of the patriarchal heritage of the Semitic tradition, in contrast to the recognition of a female element in divinity in Hinduism. The Word was 'made flesh' in a Jewish home in Palestine at a particular period in history, and the proclamation of the Gospel is inevitably in culture-related, even if not in culture-bound, terms. 'Kingdom of God', 'Messiah', 'Son of Man', 'atonement', etc., are all expressions or concepts from pre-Christian Judaism, and although they were reinterpreted in Christianity, the very use of the word 'reinterpret' implies some continuity with the original concept. How, then, can Christians disentangle the revelation of God from the Christian religion?

Another approach to emerge from missionary circles, but radically different from neo-orthodoxy, is the one known as Christian Presence. It owes much to the thinking of Bishop Kenneth Cragg, who spent many years working in Muslim lands, and who wrote the first volume of a series called 'Christian Presence amid ...'[6] The authors of the books in this series were in the main missionaries, and the general editor, M. A. C. Warren, had been a missionary in Africa before becoming General Secretary of the Church Missionary Society.[7]

The Christian Presence approach starts from the premise that the Christian does not have to 'take' God to other peoples. He is already there. God has created every man in his own image, and no one is outside his love or his saving purpose. He addresses every man and every man has the capacity to respond to him. As Max Warren says in his introduction to the Christian Presence series: 'When we approach a man of another faith

[6] *Sandals at the Mosque. Christian Presence amid Islam.* S.C.M. Press 1959.
[7] Another important volume in the series is *The Primal Vision. Christian Presence amid African Religion.* 1963. It was written by John V. Taylor, who succeeded Max Warren as General Secretary of the Church Missionary Society.

106

than our own it will be in a spirit of expectancy to find how God has been speaking to him and what new understanding of the peace and love of God we may ourselves discover in this encounter ... We have, then, to ask what is the authentic religious content in the experience of the Muslim, the Hindu, the Buddhist, or whoever he may be.'

The reference to the 'authentic religious content' in the experience of adherents of other faiths points us to another development in Christian theology. Many of the attempts to wrestle with the problem of the exclusiveness of Christianity, particularly that form of exclusiveness which maintained that salvation was only through membership of the Church, had concentrated on seeing how men of other religions could be saved *in spite of* their religion. The high moral standards of a man's life, or his spiritual qualities, were taken as an indication that he was a Christian without knowing it, that he would have responded to Christ if he had had the opportunity. The emphasis in more recent thinking has been on the possibility of a man being saved *in and through* his religion, not just in spite of it.

We are running the risk here, as in all brief summaries, of over-simplifying the position. Interest in the actual non-Christian religions rather than just in individuals is certainly a feature of recent thinking, but it would be wrong to suggest that it is completely new. In 1913, for instance, J. N. Farquhar published a book called *The Crown of Hinduism*.[8] It is a detailed study of Hinduism, designed to show that the profoundest religious insights in Hinduism find their fulfilment only in Christ. His chapter on Hindu asceticism, for example, ends with a section headed 'Christ's method of creating servants of humanity completes the Hindu ascetic discipline', and the chapter on the use of images ends with 'Christ, the image of God, satisfies these aspirations and needs in spiritual ways'. Farquhar concludes his book with the statement that in Christ is 'focused every ray of light that shines in Hinduism. He is the crown of the Faith of India'.

We shall take as an illustration of recent thinking about the way in which other religions find their fulfilment in Christ, a book called *The Unknown Christ of Hinduism*, by Raymond

[8] Second edition. Oriental Books Reprint Corporation, New Delhi 1971.

Panikkar.[9] This is a particularly interesting study because Panikkar is one of an increasing number of Christian scholars who bring to the task of doing theology the insights of non-Western cultures. He is a professor of religious studies in the University of California, Santa Barbara. He is a Roman Catholic priest, but his father was a Hindu, and he has worked in the universities of Mysore and Benares in India.

Unlike Farquhar, Panikkar does not see Hinduism as a religious system which provides only a distorted and debased vehicle for the expression of the profound religious yearning of Hindus. Instead, he describes it as a 'positive religion'. He links it with Christianity in the expression 'Hinduism and Christianity', and says: 'Our "and" certainly represents a tension ... but at the ultimate level at which it is given to us to surmise the divine will, we are bound to recognize that this "and" should not merely be interpreted in the sense of integration, assimilation or conversion, but in a higher way which does not deny the previous one.'[10] Panikkar points out that Thomas Aquinas accomplished a synthesis of Aristotle's philosophy with Christian theology, without destroying or denying the value of Aristotelian thinking, and he suggests that a synthesis of Christian theology with Hindu philosophy is actually more appropriate than the synthesis with Aristotelian philosophy.

Panikkar speaks of Hinduism being 'converted to Christ'. This does not mean the conversion of Hindus to Christianity. A quotation from another of Panikkar's writings shows us how he understands the concept of conversion. He directs our attention back to the history of Christianity, by describing it as a 'complex Hebrew-Helleno-Greco-Latino-Celtico-Gothico-Modern religion *converted* to Christ more or less successfully'.[11]

Panikkar's theology is christocentric. He says that Hinduism and Christianity meet in Christ. Christ is already in Hinduism; he is the fulfilment of Hinduism, not in the sense of crowning it, but because he has from the beginning been active in it.

A suggestion that a theocentric rather than a christocentric approach is the only way out of the theological impasse has been made by John Hick, a professor of theology in the University

[9] Darton, Longman and Todd 1964.
[10] p. 64.
[11] 'The Relation of Christians to their Non-Christian Surroundings', in Joseph Neuner, ed., *Christian Revelation and World Religions* (Burns and Oates 1967), p. 169.

of Birmingham. In his book *God and the Universe of Faiths*,[12] Hick outlines what he calls a Copernican revolution in theology. He uses the analogy of the Copernican revolution in astronomy. In the old Ptolemaic system men believed that the earth was at the centre of the universe, and that all the stars and the planets circled round it, but increasing knowledge of astronomy revealed that the movement of the planets could not be fitted exactly into this system. The problem was solved, temporarily, by suggesting that each of the planets also moved in smaller circles, while revolving round the earth, but more and more of these 'epicycles' had to be added to account for astronomical observations. When Copernicus and Galileo showed that the sun was at the centre of the universe, and everything else, including the earth, revolved round it, the whole unwieldy Ptolemaic system was discarded.

Hick describes as 'epicycles' the attempts (some of which we have noted) to maintain the uniqueness of Christianity and yet to allow that non-Christians can be saved. He believes that the only solution is to scrap the 'Ptolemaic' system of theology, as we have scrapped the Ptolemaic system of astronomy. The Copernican revolution in theology 'involves a shift from the dogma that Christianity is at the centre to the realization that it is *God* who is at the centre, and that all the religions of mankind, including our own, serve and revolve around him'.[13] Because God is infinite, he transcends man's understanding, and the religions differ because they are man's apprehension of God's revelation of himself in different cultures.

Hick points out that it is possible to operate the Ptolemaic system of theology from within any religion, and that in fact Advaita Vedantists, in Hinduism, do exactly that. We referred earlier (page 62) to Shankara's contention that devotion to God in Hinduism was only a partial approximation to the truth. Man would have to pass beyond that stage to a realization of the impersonal quality of the Absolute, Brahman. Modern Vedantists extend Shankara's reference beyond Hinduism to include all religions. They see the good Christian, for example, as an 'anonymous' Vedantist. Although he does not know it, his religious aspirations will eventually find their fulfilment in the Vedānta.

Hick's Copernican revolution in theology has not been

[12] Macmillan 1973.
[13] Hick, op. cit., p. 131.

welcomed unreservedly by other Christian theologians. At first sight it appears to offer a neat solution to the problem, but is the issue quite as straightforward as it sounds? It has been said that 'Christianity is Christ' in a way in which one would not say that 'Buddhism is Gotama' or 'Islam is Muhammad'. As we saw both in the previous chapter and earlier in this one, the role of Christ in Christianity is not just as the communicator of God's revelation. He is part of the content of the Christian faith; he is, in fact, crucial to it. Christians would therefore find it particularly problematic to have to concede the absoluteness of Christ in the way that Hick's suggestion demands.

We have in this section touched on only a few of the issues involved in the Christian theology of religions. It is a large and complex subject, and it is increasingly occupying the attention of theologians. The whole question is raised more acutely for those who are involved in inter-faith dialogue, and it is to this encounter that we turn for our last chapter.

10

DIALOGUE

We are including this postscript on interfaith dialogue, even though it is not strictly part of the study of religions, not only because those who are interested enough to undertake such a study are likely to be those who are most interested in dialogue, but also because many of the issues which have been raised throughout this book are focused in a particularly urgent way when we meet adherents of other religions face to face.

The word 'dialogue' is used in a number of different ways. Sometimes it is used loosely to refer to any kind of meeting or talking with people, but basically it is a positive encounter between people who stand within traditions which are separated by what appears to be an unbridgeable gulf. In the field of religion, for example, we have had Anglican–Roman Catholic dialogue and Christian–Marxist dialogue.

Unlike the academic study of religions, dialogue involves commitment. It is a meeting of people who are committed to a particular tradition. Only Jews and Christians can enter into Jewish–Christian dialogue. A non-religious person can meet adherents of different religions and talk with them, but he cannot be a partner in interfaith dialogue, any more than a person who is neither a Marxist nor a Christian can take part in Marxist–Christian dialogue.

Interfaith dialogue in any officially organized form is a comparatively recent phenomenon. A contributor to a symposium called *Living Faiths and the Ecumenical Movement* chronicles ecumenical activity in this area.[1] His survey begins with the World Council of Churches consultation at Davos in Switzerland in 1955, on 'Christianity and Non-Christian Religions', the issue which had been raised so dramatically at Tambaram in 1938 (see page 105). Reports, consultations and study projects succeeded each other over the years, with two important steps forward being taken in 1960—the first official interfaith meet-

[1] S. J. Samartha, ed. (W.C.C. 1971), ch. 14.

ing, between Hindus and Christians—and in 1968—the appointment of a World Council of Churches staff member, Dr S. J. Samartha, to be directly concerned with relationships between the Christian Churches and other living faiths.

The survey describes the first official multilateral dialogue, which brought together Hindus, Buddhists, Christians and Muslims at Ajaltoun, in the Lebanon, in 1970,[2] but it was written before the second multilateral consultation took place. This meeting, in 1974, with the title 'Towards World Community', was held at Colombo, in Sri Lanka. Not only did it have larger delegations from the non-Christian religions than there had been at Ajaltoun, but there were Jewish participants as well as Hindus, Buddhists, Christians and Muslims. Some indication of what this experience meant to the participants can be gained from the final paragraph of their account of the consultation:

We came to Colombo from the four corners of the globe with sometimes widely differing expectations. Our living together in community stengthened in each of us the shared readiness to reach out beyond ourselves and our several traditions in the quest for a meaningful encounter with people of living faiths and ideologies. It has helped us to compare, criticize and correlate our visions of that aspired world community which was the subject of our deliberations.[3]

There is now an increasing number of bodies concerned with interfaith dialogue. Some like the Centre for the Study of Islam and Christian–Muslim Relations (at Selly Oak in Birmingham), or the European Standing Conference of Jews, Christians and Muslims, concentrate on specific religions; others, like the World Congress of Faiths or the World Council of Churches, have a more general brief. One of the most interesting developments has been the creation by the Roman Catholic Church of a Secretariat for Non-Christians. This was instituted by Pope Paul VI in 1964 as a result of the discussions at the Second Vatican Council (see page 74). Its aim is not only to organize study and dialogue based on Rome, but to stimulate churches in

[2] See S. J. Samartha, ed., *Dialogue between Men of Living Faiths* (W.C.C. 1971), a collection of the papers presented at Ajaltoun.

[3] 'Towards World Community' (*Study Encounter*, vol. X, no. 3, 1974. W.C.C.).

different parts of the world to enter into dialogue with non-Christians. The Secretariat's activities are varied, but one particular activity of the Section on Islam will serve to illustrate its approach. Every year, at the time of the Muslim feast of Īd al-Fitr, which marks the end of Ramadān, Vatican Radio broadcasts greetings in Arabic and other languages to Muslim communities throughout the world.

A small but highly significant amount of interfaith dialogue has been undertaken independently by individuals. We mentioned earlier two Roman Catholic priests who spent a considerable time in India, living with Hindus (see page 56). This is a completely different kind of encounter from the official consultation. It is at a profound spiritual level, concerned less with expressed beliefs than with what Abhishiktānanda called 'dialogue in the cave of the heart'. This kind of dialogue will inevitably be limited to a few people who have progressed far on the spiritual pilgrimage and who have the time and opportunity to withdraw for a period from the routine demands of ordinary life, but through their writings we are able to glimpse something of the depth of their experience.

AT THE GRASSROOTS

The kind of dialogue we have considered so far has been undertaken by experts and it has involved relatively few people, but interfaith dialogue is increasingly involving 'ordinary' people. This has been happening for some time in several Asian countries, where the Christian Study Centres, established under the auspices of the World Council of Churches, have had to wrestle with the very practical problem of how Christians living alongside men of other faiths could develop positive relationships with them without compromising their own faith. It has also been happening more recently in Britain, particularly in areas where there are communities of people from non-Christian religions. Sometimes a local church has taken the initiative in bringing Christians and non-Christians together, sometimes a community relations officer or other individual has helped to create opportunities for bilateral or multilateral dialogue.

This is a completely new experience for most people, and it can be a bewildering experience. What is expected of us? What do we expect of our partners in dialogue? How do we combine commitment to our own faith with respect for the faith of others? Some people view dialogue with apprehension; they feel threatened by it. Not everyone is able to view it in the way a little Irish nun did, as Muslims, Jews and Christians arrived at the Roman Catholic conference centre where she lived. 'Oh, well,' she said, 'the good Lord will just have to sort us all out.'

Some people believe that they should be converting adherents of other faiths, not entering into dialogue with them. They see dialogue as a betrayal of their own faith. A particular verse from the Bible is frequently quoted by Christians to support this belief: 'There is no salvation in anyone else at all, for there is no other name under heaven granted to men, by which we may receive salvation' (Acts 4.12). This provides an interesting illustration of two points we considered earlier. First, the 'proof-text' is quoted out of its context (see page 61). Peter, in addressing the Jewish Sanhedrin, was not talking about world religions. The debate was *within* Judaism, and centred on the question whether Jesus was God's Messiah or not. Secondly, although the exclusivist approach can certainly be supported from the Bible, a more open approach can also be supported from it. (See pages 102f.)

What demands does interfaith dialogue make on those who take part in it? In the first place, it demands a positive attitude towards people of other religious traditions. Negative attitudes result in confrontation, not dialogue. This does not mean, however, that we have to deny our faith or water it down. Just the opposite, in fact. Dialogue is an attempt to discover the deepest and most significant beliefs of the other, and to allow the other to discover one's own deepest and most significant beliefs. It is a meeting of faith with faith.

It demands knowledge. It would be both foolish and insulting to enter into a dialogue situation without making a serious effort to understand the other person's religion. But it also demands an openness, a willingness to listen, to hear what the other is *actually* saying, not just what we expect him to be saying. We have to let him speak of the things in his religion which *he* regards as important, not just ask him about the things which *we* think are important.

But what do we hope for—or fear—from the experience? There would be no point in dialogue if nothing happened as a result of it. Is it just a greater understanding of other religions

114

that we seek, so that there may be more tolerance and less conflict in the world? That is certainly one of the results of dialogue. Is it a greater insight into our own faith? That is another result of dialogue. Are we prepared to be changed in any radical way? Do we secretly want the other person to be changed, but not ourselves? Dialogue is a searching experience, and there are no easy answers to the questions it raises.

We have been speaking of interfaith dialogue as if it were an encounter between one religion and another, but who, even at the level of the experts, let alone at grassroots level, speaks for a religion as a whole? We recognized in earlier chapters the tremendous variations which are to be found in any religion, and this is a reminder that dialogue is always between Jews and Christians, between Hindus and Buddhists, never between Judaism and Christianity, or Hinduism and Buddhism. What we encounter through dialogue is the faith of individuals, *their* apprehension of the religious tradition within which they stand, and of the ultimate reality which is the ground of their faith.

There is, however, an encounter between religions which could be described as dialogue in the broadest sense. Religions are never static. (See Chapter 7.) Among the many factors which contribute to their development is contact with other religions. In some instances this has been a negative experience, and the effect has been a defensive reaction. The relations of Christianity and Islam at the time of the crusades is an example of such an encounter. But there are also many instances of a more positive influence, with religions adopting and adapting beliefs and practices from other traditions. Hinduism, with its almost unlimited powers of absorption, is the most obvious illustration of this, and the Hindu reform movements of the past century, largely influenced by the presence of Christianity in India,[4] are a recent example of the kind of syncretism which has been characteristic of the religion through its long history.

Hinduism glories in its inclusiveness, but the word 'syncretism' has always had a bad press in Christian circles. Nevertheless, history shows that the Christian faith has also been syncretistic. It has adopted and adapted beliefs and practices from other traditions, ranging from the customs associated with Christmas to the categories of Greek philosophy in which much of Christian

[4] See M. M. Thomas, *The Acknowledged Christ of the Indian Renaissance*. S.C.M. Press 1969.

doctrine is expressed. Raymond Panikkar's delightful description (see page 108) underlines the extent to which different religions and cultures have shared in the shaping of Christianity in the past, but what of the future?

One direction in which we might look for development is interfaith dialogue. The kind of dialogue situations which we have described in this chapter will obviously prepare the ground, but a significant contribution will certainly be made by those Christian theologians in different countries who, because of their heritage, stand in a unique relationship to two living faiths. In the previous chapter we noted the contribution which men like Panikkar were making to the Christian theology of religions, but they are also beginning to influence the development of Christian theology through their attempts to bring the insights of another religion to bear on Christian doctrine. In *The Unknown Christ of Hinduism*, for example, Panikkar explores the subject of God and the world, not by trying to fit Hindu and Christian ideas together into some kind of amalgam, but by using both the Indian philosophical tradition and the Christian philosophical tradition to study a subject which, as he points out, belongs neither to the East nor to the West.

Any form of interfaith dialogue confronts Christians with the kind of questions which have been discussed in these last two chapters, but, looked at purely from the point of view of the study of religions, it provides a fascinating illustration in our own century of the factors which contribute to change. The religions of the world are in closer contact than they have ever been in the past. What effect will they have on one another? As we look back in history we can see the ways in which religions have developed, but the process of change is a continuous one—and we are now not merely spectators of it, we are part of it. Some development there will certainly be in the coming decades. What direction will it take?

INDEX

117